Single Adult Ministry for Today

Bobbie Reed, Ph.D.

SAINT LOUIS

The Bible learning activities in Chapter 4 are reprinted from *Creative Bible Learning for Adults* by Monroe Marlowe and Bobbie Reed. Copyright © 1977 by Regal Books, Ventura, CA 93003. Used by permission.

Scripture taken from the HOLY BIBLE, NEW INTERNATIONAL VERSION®. NIV®. Copyright © 1973, 1978, 1984 by International Bible Society. Used by permission of Zondervan Publishing House. All rights reserved.

Copyright ©1996 Concordia Publishing House
3558 S. Jefferson Avenue, St. Louis, MO 63118-3968
Manufactured in the United States of America

Library of Congress Cataloging-in-Publication Data

Reed, Bobbie.
    Single adult ministry for today / Bobbie Reed.
       p.   cm.
     ISBN 0-570-04840-0
     1. Church work with single people—United States. 2. Lutheran Church—Missouri Synod—Membership. 3. Lutheran Church—United States—Membership. I. Title.
    BV639.S5R44   1996
    259`.08`652—dc20   95-23858

1 2 3 4 5 6 7 8 9 10   03 02 01 00 99 98 97 96 95 96

Contents

Part I

Minister with Single Adults

chapter 1

KNOW YOUR SINGLE ADULTS

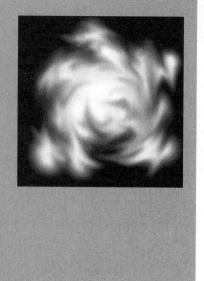

If you are a single adult, or a person interested in ministering with single adults, you will want to be sure that you have a thorough understanding of single adults and the challenges they face in daily life. Even if you are single yourself, there may be aspects of singleness that are foreign to your experience or that you may never have considered. As you prepare to minister, or to begin coordinating a ministry, check your understanding of the realities of being a modern single adult.

UNDERSTAND THE STAGES OF AGES

All single adults are not alike! Big surprise, right? But have you taken the time to notice just what the differences are? First, there are age-level differences.

Undeniable differences exist between generations, yet you will have single adults from several generations who may attend your ministry. Seek to understand the differences in the generational stages, then the differences in individual single adults. The following is a brief summary of age groups, titles/labels, and characteristics as outlined by current researchers.[1] You will begin to see the exciting possibilities as you welcome representatives of each group in your single adult ministry.

Persons born before 1915 are considered "elderly"

A person born before 1915 was at least 80 years old in 1995. When these single adults were growing up, getting married was something "everyone did" or was expected to do. Therefore, these single adults have usually been married at some time in their lives. They may have spent their younger years committed to a strong work ethic, believing that one had better give everything to a job to keep it. They believe that delayed gratification is the best choice because when you least expect it, the bottom may fall out. They may have things at home they've never used because "saving for a rainy day" may be a lifelong habit. Remember, these people were young when the Depression hit, and they know what it is like to do without. They may resist change and upgrading the quality of ministry—"It's been good enough for 20 years; we don't need something new now."

Older adults may have transportation difficulties, health problems, serious financial limitations, and may experience acute loneliness. Some can get preoccupied with the reality of death as birthdays add up and close friends die.

But individuals in this age group are unique and can be invaluable to a minister/leader in single adult ministry. These single adults usually hold to traditional values and morals. Because of their longevity, they have developed a broader life perspective than someone who is very young. Their experiences and memories are resources they can draw upon when faced with new problems or situations. Their sense of history, both of the world and of your own church (if they are long-time members), is valuable. Often older adults are more mellow than younger singles and tend to fly off the handle less frequently. They may have developed genuine wisdom. Some have spent their lives studying God's Word. His light shines in them. A wise minister/leader in single adult ministry will draw upon such "elderly" single adults as advisors, mentors, sounding boards, listeners, and as people from whom to learn.

Persons born between 1915 and 1926 are called "the new elders"

Persons born between 1915 and 1926 were between the ages of 69 and 80 in 1995. Because the expectation of "marriage as normal" still existed in the young adult years of this age group, these single adults have also usually been married for at least part of their lives. They also tend to have bought into the belief in the work ethic and have little patience with persons who don't pull their weight, who are lazy, or who don't take care of themselves or their families.

Some new elders will be in poor health, but many will be surprisingly spry and ready to maintain an active social life and be involved in ministry. They need to be involved, listened to, and valued.

This group can provide a unique perspective and support to the ministry. Those who have grown in personal and spiritual maturity possess many of the same characteristics as the "elderly" single adult. Because this group is younger, they can be more active in ministry. In this group, you may find excellent teachers, idea persons, and people who have learned through life experiences how best to resolve differences between individuals or between groups of people. Perhaps they also can serve as "adoptive grandparents" for some of the children of single parents, or even for single adults in their early 20s. Those who can't be physically active in the ministry can contribute by writing letters, sending cards, and telephoning visitors and members.

Persons born between 1927 and 1945 have been designated as "boosters" by some sociologists

Single adults born between 1927 and 1945 were between 50 and 68 in

1995. The term "boosters" is used because they serve as stabilizers in the 1990s and tend to support the "American dream," traditional institutions, cultural beliefs, and family values. Other sociologists and researchers have designated this group as "younger new elders," "the Eisenhower Generation," or the "G. I. Generation." These single adults are often characterized as conformists—people who work hard, do their share, don't rock the boat, cooperate, and try to make everyone happy. Most of these people have also been married at some time in their lives.

Boosters need acceptance; encouragement to risk reaching out to new experiences and people and to set and achieve life-changing goals; affirmation for their contributions; and a place for fellowship.

This group can contribute a lot to single adult ministry. Those who have worked through their own developmental "passages" are in a "contented" stage of life, yet they still display a level of excitement and energy that can be contagious. You will have many in this group who are past their mid-life crises and are ready to move into the next phase of life with hope and expectation. In this group, you will find people who are committed to a strong work ethic. They will be willing to continue working in ministry doing those tasks that may be boring but need to be done. They tend not to need glamour, up-front recognition, or attention, and many are ready to work behind the scenes. Usually they are interested in learning and are supportive of your educational activities.

Because of their life experiences, those boosters who have clung to Christ through bitterness and struggles will be helpful to you in finding solutions to problems, reinforcing values and standards, and encouraging others in the faith. Therefore, you will draw from such individuals when you need advisors and mentors for younger single adults or those who seem to be stuck in a developmental stage or one of the destructive stages of divorce or grief recovery. These people also are helpful because they have personal initiative, are willing to work on the nitty-gritty aspects of the ministry, and are willing to make personal sacrifices to ensure the success of a project to which they are committed. You will find single adults in this group who have good planning skills and who are mature leaders.

Persons born between 1946 and 1964 are commonly called "baby boomers"

Baby boomers (persons between the ages of 31 and 49 in 1995) are divided into "early boomers" and "late boomers," depending on their dates of birth. This generation has received a tremendous amount of media attention and publicity. Basically, this is a consumer generation, raised by parents who wanted their children to have more than they did and who worked hard to give their children everything. Boomers grew up expecting life to give them from its abundance, and for the most part, it did.

Boomers grew up optimistic. They knew (and proved it true) that if one worked hard, one would be promoted and could earn a high salary. They expected to go to college, and many did. They expected to be able to own their own homes, and the housing industry flourished. Interest rates soared. The economy was healthy. The American dream came true for those who learned how to work the system.

Boomers want things bigger and better, and they are willing to work to earn the money to get what they want. They are, as a result of what our culture created for them, often more individualistic than group-oriented. They prefer short-term commitments rather than lifelong decisions. They may change jobs, marriage partners, careers, and goals with ease and frequency.

A ministry with single adults in this age group must be designed to address these issues. Instead of a traditional 13-week study, attendance will be better for four- to six-week classes. Instead of making commitments to become missionaries forever, short-term mission trips and projects are preferred. The quality of the printed material, the program, the sound system, the meeting place, the speakers, and the music is expected to be high. If it isn't, don't expect these single adults to stick around too long.

Boomers are fun! Those who have combined the above characteristics with a strong personal faith in Christ, as well as a sense of fairness and personal maturity, will be some of your strongest leaders and helpers. Because they believe in the "can do" approach and are confident, dedicated, reliable, and competent workers for a cause they believe in, such individuals will become the backbone of your leadership structure. The combination of strong optimism and logical perspective, along with a biblical foundation and practical theology, makes for someone you will want heading up new ministry areas, taking the lead on projects, being in charge of records and reports, teaching classes translating principles into understandable concepts, and taking on demanding leadership roles.

Persons born after 1964 are known as "baby busters"

Busters (those single adults under age 31 in 1995) are called that partly because they were born when the birth rate was roughly half of what it had been during the post-World War II baby boom.

Busters are very different from boomers. Their world has caused them to become a generation of pessimistic adults. Jobs are just not as available as they once were. Coming in at entry level and being promoted because of hard work is no longer a reality. The opportunities for individual entrepreneurship are no longer as promising as they were for boomers. Small businesses fail daily. States pass rules and regulations that make starting your own business extremely risky and success unlikely. Buying a home on a beginner's salary is virtually impossible.

Therefore, busters are convinced that no matter how hard they work, they still may not make it, so they expect their parents to help out. (This is usually a major expectation, and the "help" they expect may run into the thousands of dollars. To them, this is reasonable. To their parents, it's unthinkable.) They may live at home longer and put off marrying because they don't like the world they have inherited. They are not ready to leave the nest. Often those who do move out on their own return home one or more times before making a successful transition.

On the other hand, busters have been raised in a world of quality, electronics, gadgets, and high expectations. Consequently, their wants and dreams are way beyond their means. A ministry with these single adults must be contemporary, glitzy, electronically sophisticated, and high quality, yet affordable!

Still, busters need love, acceptance, companionship, assistance, recovery programs, and most of all, hope.

A ministry with busters is anything but boring—it's hyper-exciting! Those who are not caught in hopelessness and helplessness bring a sense of energetic enthusiasm, an eye for quality, a flexibility that is undaunted by any setback, a readiness to make changes, and an eclectic acceptance of a variety of approaches and ideas. They are risk takers. They like to be involved and do things for themselves (although they still like to be served). They understand that God is their only hope and make personal commitments to follow Jesus.

A wise minister/leader taps into the strengths of this age group for energy and high payoff, providing recognition for achievement. This group will undoubtedly come up with creative ideas. And they will provide you honest feedback about what is and isn't working.

Persons born after 1982 have not yet been labeled

These people are not yet single *adults*, but they will form an identity of their own. They will be joining your single adult ministries around the year 2001.

The challenge you face is to design and develop a ministry with single adults that will effectively minister to each of the different stages of ages.

UNDERSTAND DIFFERENCES IN SINGLE ADULTS BY STATUS

Several types of single adults may attend your church and are potential participants in a ministry with singles.

Single adults who have not been married

"But Mother, I'm not ready to get married now. I like my life just as it is. I have a great job and can come and go as I please. I enjoy the company of several close friends, men and women," Jan argued. "It is really okay to be single! Maybe I'll decide to get married later, but not right now!"

The *single* adult who has never married may be a young person of college age or a little older. Or the single adult may be someone of any age who has remained single, either by choice or lack of opportunity. Today, single adults are waiting longer to marry than they did 30 years ago. In the 1960s, a person who was not at least engaged by the time college was over was either an object of pity or suspicion!

In the 1990s, we recognize that some single adults choose not to marry at all. Some choose to wait until their careers are settled or until they have reached other goals. However, a coupled society is frequently suspicious of the single adult who is not eager to marry. The not-too-subtle implication is that there must be something "wrong" with the person. It is important for us to accept those who, for one reason or another, choose not to marry. In some cases, that choice is the wise one.

Single adults who have never been married may question their self-worth and wrestle with issues of rejection, identity, acceptance of the single status, and building friendships and relationships to take the place of family relationships. They often have to face and learn to deal with prejudices. (Is there a question of sexual orientation? Are they after someone's spouse? Is there something secretly, terribly wrong with them?)

The single person is hurt by insinuating questions such as:

- "Aren't you perhaps a bit too picky?"
- "What's the matter with you? Don't you want the responsibility of becoming a parent?"
- "I guess you are just having too much fun to get married, huh?"
- "Do you plan on remaining single for the rest of your life?"
- "Why do you let all of the good ones get away?"
- "What have you got against marriage?"
- "Aren't you ever going to settle down and get serious about living and get married?"

We must learn to accept singleness as an "okay" status in and of itself. Being single offers a great degree of freedom and the opportunity to be independent and totally in control of one's choices. Single people can be available for ministry options because they are not bound to a spouse whose needs and desires must be considered. The apostle Paul said that being single can be a gift from and for God.

The single adult who has never been married needs acceptance, encouragement, affirmation, challenge, and a safe environment to develop self-esteem, direction, self-acceptance, and to grow and mature spiritually.

It's exciting to work with and be around people who are single and satisfied (at least for the time being). They have the freedom to make commitments to ministry, mission trips, or financial giving without considering the impact on spouse or children. Many of these single adults are energetic, available, free, fun, and committed to the Lord's work. They have lots of friends because they have developed the ability to recognize and appreciate the strengths of different people.

A wise minister/leader will look to these single adults to participate in mission projects/trips, plan active social events (beach parties, ski retreats, volleyball nights), share their experiences in learning to live for Christ as a single adult, or take on campus outreach activities.

Single again by divorce

"You what?" Nancy exclaimed incredulously.

"I want a divorce," Bob repeated in a quiet, defeated voice.

"I don't believe it. I just can't believe it." Nancy shook her head as if to stop her whirling thoughts. The last few weeks had been rough, but she and Bob had survived rough times before.

A month later Bob moved out and filed for divorce. Five months later, Nancy (and Bob) were single again.

Divorced persons, newly single again, are typically hurting and in some stage of the grieving process. They may still be in shock, denial, or bargaining. They may be stuck in depression or anger. They need assistance, comfort, love, acceptance, hugs, friendship, and a safe place to come and be with other people.

After a while, most divorced persons realize they must forgive the past, themselves, and their former spouse. They move on to acceptance and hope. They still need the same loving, welcoming attitude and friendship as before, but they are less desperate and fragile. Therefore, they benefit from the challenge to let go of the past and look forward to all God has in store for them.

There is no right time frame for a person to recover from the divorce experience. Some people are "emotionally divorced" long before the legal divorce occurs. Therefore, they complete their emotional mourning years before the actual separation. Others are shocked by the divorce, without a clue anything is *that* wrong in the marriage. Some are admittedly relieved to be out of a bad marriage. Others don't want to let go of the idea of being married and refuse to accept their status as a single-again adult. Some remarry quickly to resolve their conflict with singleness.

Just as being in love and walking down a church aisle does not a successful married couple make, neither does being unhappy and walking out of a divorce court a successful single-again make. Both adjustments take time and work.

It is exciting to work with single adults who have recovered from the pain of divorce and have learned valuable lessons in the process. These persons can be strong resources because they have a unique awareness of the pain of rejection and divorce, information about the legalities involved, and personal experience of the healing process. Many divorced persons express a strong faith in God and hope for the future. They usually have improved their skills in relating to others as friends and even as partners.

Therefore, a wise minister/leader will use these people as facilitators for divorce recovery groups, teachers, peer counselors, telephone counselors, helpers for single parents, and prayer partners. Good leaders, mentors, and workers are included in this group.

Single again by death of a spouse

"She's dead." The doctor's quiet words sounded like a cruel shout in the hospital waiting room.

"Oh, God!" Sam cried, suddenly single again. "What am I going to do now?"

Widowed persons experience many of the same problems, hurts, and grieving processes as divorced persons. They lose a spouse as well as coupled status. They must develop a new identity and lifestyle. This is not an easy task. Familiar habits and roles are no longer appropriate. Widowed persons must make new decisions and reestablish themselves in a society so obviously designed for couples.

Widowed persons also need acceptance, a safe place to talk about their departed spouse, love, support, attention, and a gentle challenge to put their lives back together.

People who have lost a spouse by death, who have worked through the grief cycle and have come through strengthened in their faith, have a lot to offer your ministry. Their personal knowledge of grief and pain, hope and recovery, is valuable as they reach out to help others. Also, because many of the widowed had good marriage relationships with their spouses, some of them can teach relationship skills, the art of compromising, and the finer aspects of communication.

A wise minister/leader knows when to use these people as counselors, teachers, mentors, and support-group leaders, in addition to other roles suited to their special gifts or abilities.

Single parents

"How am I supposed to raise my two sons alone?" Patti asked the therapist angrily. "I don't know how! I never was a little boy."

Some single and single-again adults are parents. Some parents have sole custody, some joint custody, some visitation rights only, and some have no contact with their children, either by their own choice or because of the choice of the other parent.

Each type of single parent faces hurts, challenges, frustrations, and regrets. Some are still struggling with their own pain but have to be emotionally strong to help the children through the fallout of the divorce or the aftermath of losing a parent by death. Some single parents also have learned to experience the joys of parenthood and to face each new day with excitement.

Single parents need acceptance, help with parenting, physical and practical assistance, respite, encouragement, affirmation, and all the love you can give.

Single parents, of necessity, often develop a strong practical sense about how to do five things at once and how to set priorities when making choices. They often find moments of joy in the middle of chaos and confusion. Such people are valuable and can assist a minister/leader in working with other single parents and in sharing parenting and practical ideas.

While there are many similarities in the needs of the different types of single adults, there are significant differences also. It will be a challenge to design and develop an effective ministry with single adults who come from these different groups.

Be aware that the characteristics, strengths, and needs described for single adults in various age stages, as well as different single status types, are generalizations only! A single adult may be more properly characterized by an age stage other than the one in which his birthday places him. A single adult does not always fit into the status category her life situation specifies. These generalizations are to be used as guidelines only and not as strict categorizations.

UNDERSTAND THE SINGLE ADULTS IN YOUR COMMUNITY

As you seek to understand the differences and similarities among the single adults in your church, you will also want to ask: What is unique in this community that impacts the lives of single adults?

★ Is yours primarily a college town, or is your church near a major college or university? Are the majority of single adults living within five miles of your church college students?

★ Has a major employer in the area just closed its doors, moved out of state, or gone through a significant "downsizing" that has left many adults (both single and married) out of work?

★ Is yours a "beach community"? A street-gang-dominated neighborhood? A middle-class, family suburb? A military base and support city?

Take a look at the community and be aware of what pressures, interests, and issues are impacting the single adults with whom you want to minister. This is important information to consider as you plan your ministry.

When Jesus walked the earth during His ministry, He often addressed the issues of the day and of the community. He talked easily with the Samaritan woman at the well. He spoke in the temple, taught in the synagogues, and walked the countryside communicating with people who gathered around Him. He was flexible in His approach to reaching people. Jesus spoke in parables, fed the multitudes with compassion, and healed the sick who came to Him for help. He assured sinners that their sins were forgiven. He dealt with people at all levels, on all levels. Jesus knew the community to which He ministered.

RECOGNIZE THE MYTHS ABOUT SINGLE ADULTS

"You're not getting me to go to a singles' group," Kevin asserted. "I'm not that desperate!"

There are myths about almost every phase of singleness and about single adult ministries. As a minister/leader with single adults, it is important to become familiar with the myths and help eliminate them from the thinking of church members. What makes myths believable is that some of them are true some of the time. Therefore, when people see something about a single adult that reinforces a stereotype, the myth is perpetuated. For example, perhaps you have heard that single adults:

- are "swingers"
- are sexually active
- are desperate to get married
- have never grown up
- are not whole people
- need to get married
- have more fun
- have a lot of freedom
- have an easy life
- like being alone
- are selfish

- have major personal and emotional problems
- are irresponsible
- are transient
- are lonely
- are a threat to married persons
- cannot be good parents
- cannot provide a good home
- do not have good relational skills.

Believing these stereotypes and perpetuating the myths can be harmful to the nurturing environment you want to develop for your ministry. Yes, some single adults might fit one or more of these statements, but the majority of them do not.

Consider What Single Adults Need

Some basic needs a single adult ministry can be designed to meet include:[2]

Belongingness

Our deepest need is to love and be loved. We have a strong need to belong, to feel accepted, and to identify with a particular group. A single adult ministry can provide this. A part of the good news of the Gospel of Jesus Christ is that believers are a part of the body of Christ. We belong. We belong to God because we were purchased by the blood of Christ (1 Peter 1:18–19). We belong to Christ because the Father has given us to Him (John 10:28–29). We belong to one another because we are members of one body.

Inherent in belonging is the concept that one is accepted. Truly accepting people is not always easy because it means relinquishing our ideas about what is right for others. Accepting people means allowing them to be where they are in their personal and spiritual journeys even if we wish they were further along in either or both. Accepting means letting people solve their own problems—within the guidance of God's Law and Gospel—even when we disagree with their solutions.

Hope

Hope is an important gift your single adults need. Hope that life can be abundant. Hope that God's plan for each person's life is perfect (Rom. 12:1–2). Hope that there is a place where people are accepted for who they are and not rejected because they aren't coupled. God has promised us that it is in the Divine will to give us a future and a hope (Jer. 29:11).

Understanding

Even though single adults can be accepted in a church as part of the entire congregation, it is helpful for them to find a place not only of acceptance but also of understanding. A place where others gather who have been through a divorce or who have lost a spouse through death. A place where they can find the gift of true comfort, where they walk alongside each other because of shared experiences (2 Cor. 1:3–5).

Role models

The leaders in your single adult ministry can provide good role models for those who attend. Models of people who have been through the valley of rejection and survived and the valley of the shadow of death and survived. Models of people who have let go of anger and are reaching out to others in love. Models of parents who are striving to make excellent homes for their children. Models of mature Christianity gained through trials and tribulations and trusting by faith. The eleventh chapter of Hebrews is an example of the role models of faith God provides. Role models are important. Don't forget to be one.

Information

Another function of your single adult ministry is providing information, for example: biblical instruction, practical assistance, seminars and workshops on relevant topics, parenting ideas, personal growth techniques, and discipleship studies for spiritual growth.

Companionship

A single adult ministry is a place where Christian single adults can come for safe companionship. Part of the companionship is fellowship, part is socializing, part is keeping loneliness at bay, and part is developing genuine friendships.

Sometimes single adults need comfort. Sometimes they need caring. And often they need a warm, friendly hug. We call this the "ministry of touch." There are times when single adults go for days at a time without ever coming into physical contact with another adult. The puppy who greets one at the door with enthusiastic licks is nice. The child who crawls up into a lap and snuggles is nice. But sometimes what people need is another adult to envelop them in a big bear hug that says, "You're safe. You're going to make it. You're not alone. I understand."

Another function of companionship is listening. We can help each other through listening. We don't have to have the answers, in fact, it is often better if we don't try to give answers. All that is required is empathetic listening. Talking is a way of clarifying ideas and making up one's mind. Sometimes as we talk through our ideas, we see the flaws in our thinking. Talking is a wonderful release. It helps people relax and unwind. Don't forget to encourage people to listen to one another.

WORD CHOICES ARE IMPORTANT

You will want to consider carefully the words you use in conjunction with your ministry. While there may not be anything terribly wrong with some words, others are preferable because of the implications given or received.

- Instead of referring to people as "singles," you may want to call them "single adults." They are not a separate species but simply adults who are single.

- Instead of referring to single adults as "never married" and "formerly married," which emphasizes marriage as a point of reference, use terms such as "single" and "single again." (In fact, Dr. Harold Ivan Smith once quipped that married persons might well be called "formerly single"!)

- Avoid referring to your "single adult *program*." Calling it your "single adult *ministry*" implies a deeper meaning and value.

  And prepositions are important also.

- A "ministry/minister *for* single adults" may imply that something is being provided for a group of people that has no input, no ownership, and no participation.

- A "ministry/minister *to* single adults" may imply that this is something done to a group of people that again has no input, no ownership, and no participation.

- A "ministry/minister *with* single adults" implies that the single adults have input, ownership, participation, and importance.

Carefully choose a title for your ministry or names for your classes. Don't use terms that can appear derogatory. Years ago this was a problem in many single adult groups. In one church, the single adults called themselves "The Other Group." Titles such as "Unclaimed Blessings" and "Pairs and Spares" convey a negative message.

Whatever words you use in your ministry, at least take the time to consider them and to choose them wisely. Follow Paul's advice in Col. 4:5–6 and be gracious in your choice of words and in your speech.

BE WISE AND UNDERSTANDING

Solomon gave good advice when he wrote, "Wisdom is supreme; therefore get wisdom. Though it cost all you have, get understanding" (Prov. 4:7).

Learn all you can about single adults. Learn all you can about ministry options. Then develop a deep sense of how to be understanding. You may not always *understand*, but you can always *be understanding*. The reasons people do certain things may escape you. You may not be able to identify with or accept the logic behind a person's choices or decisions. But you can be understanding and accepting of that person as an individual and as a valuable member of the body of Christ. You can be an understanding minister/leader with single adults, sharing in the journey, walking alongside, and caring for each person God brings to you.

CHECK YOUR UNDERSTANDING

✔ 1. Can you explain the differences between single adults in various age stages?

✔ 2. Can you explain the different reasons and circumstances some adults are single?

✔ 3. Can you identify the unique aspects of your community that may impact the single adults you hope to bring into your ministry?

✔ 4. Can you identify the ways a ministry might relate to the different single adults who come to your church?

✔ 5. Have you carefully considered the terminology you use in conjunction with your ministry plans?

If these questions have identified areas in which you need to do further investigation, take action today!

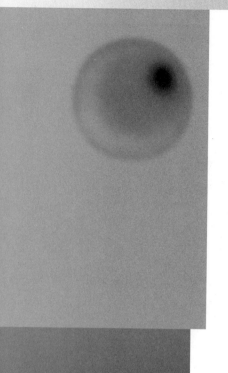

chapter 2

CLARIFY YOUR REASONS FOR MINISTRY

"We must have a single adult ministry," Deanne asserted to her pastor.

"Yes, we must. There's nothing in our current program that addresses the needs of single adults," George agreed. "Several of us single adults have talked it over, and we are ready to help get a ministry started."

The pastor set aside a meeting time, and the group of eager single adults gathered to begin planning a new ministry. However, in the course of discussion, it was soon evident that various participants had different perceptions of the need for ministry.

IDENTIFY YOUR REASONS FOR MINISTRY

The first step in planning a ministry is to be very clear about why you want a ministry with single adults. When discussing single adult ministries, pastors and church leaders often ask these questions:

- "Why single out single adults?"

- "Why do single adults need their own Sunday school classes?"

- "Why can't we just reassure single adults that we love them and fit them into our other adult programs?"

- "If we separate single adults, won't they feel isolated and rejected?"

Let's examine why churches need ministries with single adults.

- *Single adults have different needs that can be better addressed in a separate ministry with other single adults.* Sometimes recently divorced or widowed single adults are hurting and need the tenderness and acceptance of other single adults who understand, not just academically but also experientially (2 Cor. 1:3–5).

A single adult ministry is one place where the Holy Spirit can work to heal people as they reach out to others hurting because of similar experiences.

- *Some single adults are not comfortable attending a couples' Sunday school class where they are constantly reminded that they do not have a partner.* The silent reminders of what has been lost, or never experienced, hurt too much. A single adult ministry assures people that marriage is not a requirement for inclusion in the body of Christ or the work of the church.

- *A single adult ministry takes into consideration that people may not be where we wish they were in their spiritual and personal journeys.* Through ministry, we can meet people where they are, affirm them, and support them.

Appendix A presents a biblical basis for ministry with single adults and their families.

REASONS SOME CHURCHES DON'T HAVE MINISTRIES WITH SINGLE ADULTS

Although the need for a ministry with single adults is recognized in many churches across the United States, there are still some who do not have such ministries. The reasons vary.

Lack of acceptance of the need

A few church leaders believe that adults in the church need to be grouped together and not separated according to any particular need or life circumstance. Such people believe that the church does not exist to meet personal needs but only to spread the Good News of the Gospel of Jesus Christ, specifically through evangelism. Meeting personal needs is the individual's own responsibility.

This point of view ignores the approach of the early church in taking care of the widows and the poor (Acts 4:32–35; 6:1–2) and the exhortation of Paul that Christians bear one another's burdens (Gal. 6:2).

Some church leaders believe there are not enough single adults in the church or community to support a specialized ministry. This point of view ignores an important reality. A significant number of single adults live in virtually every community in our country. If single adults are not coming to a particular church, it is probably because they don't feel that the church cares about them or can help them meet their spiritual needs.

Belief that single adult ministries give the wrong message

Several misconceptions fall into this category.

Misconception #1

"If a church is truly committed to supporting the family structure and family values, then having a ministry with single adults would be incompatible. People might believe that being single or staying single-again is an acceptable alternative."

The truth is, being single *is* an acceptable alternative. Remember the teachings of the apostle Paul? (Cf. 1 Cor. 7:7–9.)

Misconception #2

"Having a separate ministry with single adults will automatically divide the church into 'marrieds' and 'singles.'"

The truth is, single adults involved in a specialized ministry are still integrated into the life of the church through participation in the choir, musical events, drama presentations, home visitations, work days, mission conferences, worship services, classes, seminars, weekday children's groups, and any number of other ways.

Misconception #3

"The single adult phenomenon will soon go away. The United States will soon embrace family values again to the point that there will be few divorces, more marriages, and the numbers of single adults will decrease so that separate ministries will be unnecessary."

If this ever occurs, then single adult ministries may indeed become less of a priority. But until such a time (which will probably never come), we can't ignore the large segment of our population that is single and single-again.

Lack of financial resources

Most churches are conscious of their budgets when considering what ministries they can support. Depending on ministry priorities, additional staff persons are hired to assist the pastor. Often a music minister, youth pastor, or a general "associate pastor" are hired before a church considers hiring a minister to work with single adults.

However, don't ignore the needs of single adults just because the budget cannot support a special minister. Many effective single adult ministries are started and efficiently run by lay leaders and volunteers. And as single adults are brought to your church, they bring additional resources in terms of energy, talents, gifts, and finances. These can help defray the cost of having a ministry.

Fear of failure

Some churches don't minister with single adults because they tried it once and were unsuccessful. Perhaps the timing wasn't right or the lay leaders weren't dedicated or trained enough. The fear of failure ought not keep a church from ministry. Instead, the fear may be a reminder that sufficient prayerful research and planning are part of preparing for a new ministry.

Often the fear of failure stems from the need to "look good" at everything. Church leaders need to remember that they don't have to excel and be the best at everything. Start small and grow a ministry tailored to your unique needs.

Theological concerns

Some people believe that having a single adult ministry means they openly condone divorce. Not true. God hates divorce (Mal. 2:16). But the divorced person is loved. Jesus ate with publicans and sinners as part of His table ministry, but He did not condone their actions because He associated with them. Instead, Jesus changed their lives. Remember Zacchaeus?

A second theological concern involves subsequent marriages of divorced persons. Many divorced persons do marry again, which is in conflict with the theological positions held by various churches. Therefore, some of those churches elect not to have single adult ministries because they believe that to do so encourages marriages they cannot condone.

While your policy of performing marriage ceremonies for divorced persons must be clarified and acknowledged, it need not prevent your church from reaching out to single adults with care and concern.

Lack of leaders for the new ministry

Ask God to prepare the hearts of the persons who will be good leaders for your group. Invite interested persons to gather to discuss the possibilities of beginning a ministry with single adults, and you will most likely see effective leadership emerge.

WRONG REASONS FOR HAVING A MINISTRY WITH SINGLE ADULTS

There might be wrong reasons to have a ministry with single adults in your church. These would include:

It's the fad to have one

If you are only developing a ministry with single adults because it is "the thing to do" as a modern church, then your ministry will probably not succeed. A ministry with single adults needs to be based on a vision for the need and a loving desire to minister.

The church down the street has one

If you are planning a ministry with single adults only because another church has one and you don't want to lose your single adults, then your ministry probably won't be effective. Ministry is not about competition.

Single adults are sick and need help

Some single adults are sick, and some need help. If your attitude toward single adults in general is that they are all deficient in some way (socially, emotionally, spiritually, mentally, relationally), then your ministry may not be loving, caring, or effective. Most single adults are healthy, and their needs are situational not developmental.

We want to keep single adults separate

If your church wants to develop a single adult ministry to keep single adults away from the rest of your church body, you have a problem. The need for a specialized ministry is not because single adults should be kept separate from the rest of the people.

As part of the process of identifying your reasons for designing and developing a ministry with single adults, you will want to list your reasons and evaluate them for appropriateness. Next, you will want to select the ministry design option that best suits your situation.

SINGLE ADULT MINISTRY OPTIONS

Let's examine four approaches to ministering with single adults.

No ministry

A church can decide not to have a separate ministry with single adults. There will be no separate Bible study, no socials or other activities designed primarily for the unmarried. This church may or may not actively seek to involve single adults in its established ministries.

For a while, this approach may seem to have few adverse consequences, unless you look closely. Those single adults who do continue to attend will come to accept as fact the implication of unconcern. They will seek to have their needs met outside the church. Eventually, some will drift away from thi church to attend another where there is an active ministry for them. They may drop out of church completely.

A social program

Some churches do not separate single adults for spiritual ministry but do acknowledge that single adults may have unique social needs. Technically, this social group operates under the name and umbrella of the church and at least the officers are required to be members of the church. However, the responsibility for planning and running the program is shouldered by group members with little or no investment by the church.

When the emphasis is social rather than spiritual, participants tend to identify with the group and with each other instead of with the church itself. The church lends its name, sanction, and facilities and provides nominal supervision. The program will continue as long as the single adults remain actively involved; it may be discontinued if interest wanes or the facilities are needed for a higher priority program.

Advantages of a social program such as this include:

- Requires little investment from the church in terms of time, energy, money, and commitment

- Provides a simple way to have a single adult program

- Keeps your single adults from going to another church in search of a single adult program

- May serve as a way to draw in single adults from the community who wouldn't come to a church service

- Allows the church to start slowly and check the possible responses to a full single adult ministry

- Encourages single adults to interact with and learn from each other

Disadvantages of just having a social program include:

- It may be only a program, not a ministry.

- There may be a lack of spiritual emphasis.

- It may not meet the spiritual needs of single adults.

- There may be a mistaken belief that the needs of single adults are being met because there is a "program" for them.

• The single adult program may be isolated from the total church program.

Carefully consider these disadvantages.

A spiritual ministry

A third option is to design a ministry with single adults that concentrates only on the spiritual issues. Little consideration is given to identifying, discussing, or dealing with the nonspiritual needs or problems of single adults. The ministry is designed to reach and evangelize single adults and assist them in banding together in shared Christian growth.

Because the emphasis is spiritual, the functions may include Sunday morning as well as weekday Bible studies, small-group discussions centering on doctrinal or theological issues, and visitation to single adults who are ill or otherwise shut in and unable to attend worship services. If there are socials or personal growth functions, these are few and given a low priority. Consequently, participants tend to identify with the church rather than with other single adults.

The level of commitment required for this type of ministry is high in the area of reaching people for Christ but low in actually ministering with single adults. Church leaders are not required to understand where single adults are coming from or what challenges they face. The program is virtually a carbon copy of other ministries for adults in the church. For example, the single adult Sunday school class uses the same curriculum as other adult classes, without any modification or adaptation to the realities of single living. In other words, single adults are considered different because they aren't married not because they have special needs. Once initiated, this type of program tends to continue whether or not the interest level of the participants rises or falls.

The advantages of a spiritual-involvement-only ministry would include:

• Requires only a minimum investment from the church in terms of time, energy, or money

• Provides a fairly simple way to have a ministry with single adults

• Keeps your single adults attending your church

• Encourages single adults to get together and enjoy and learn from one another

• Emphasizes spiritual things, Christian growth, and reaching others for Christ

• Provides a solid spiritual foundation for single adults who participate and can lead to a strong core group of those who faithfully attend

There are also a few disadvantages to this type of ministry:

• Attracts only the conservative and sincere seeker of God's Word and not all single adults

• Minimizes or ignores the very real needs and problems faced by single adults in their daily lives

• Isolates the spiritual side of people rather than assists them in integrating the biblical perspective into all aspects of life

- Ignores the entire realm of practical theology that integrates the total life experience, the church community experience, and the biblical perspective

- Discourages openness and honesty about one's personal failures that are seen as a direct result of a lack of trust in God

- Excludes the non-Christian who is looking for spiritual help but is not yet ready to embrace the faith

Once again, churches need to prayerfully consider these ideas when designing a single adult ministry limited to spiritual involvement.

A balanced ministry

The fourth alternative, and the one that is recommended as both desirable and effective, takes a balanced approach to ministry with single adults.

This approach recognizes that single adults are a unique group of people that shares special challenges and faces similar life decisions. Single adults have some basic needs that are identifiably different from those shared by adults in general and married couples in particular. A balanced ministry is designed to meet these specific needs. Opportunities are provided for personal as well as spiritual growth, for relational as well as individual development, in an atmosphere of openness, honesty, Christian love, and acceptance.

Typical functions include Sunday school classes, Bible studies, small-group discussions held during the week, socials, service projects, mission projects/trips, fellowship times, and educational opportunities as well as recovery programs. However, the calendar is carefully planned and coordinated with the church calendar so that single adults are free to attend and participate in all-church activities. Single adults are recruited as teachers, leaders, and workers in other church programs.

With this approach, single adults will identify with and feel they belong both to the church and the ministry. This type of program requires a high level of commitment. The pastor and church leaders must take time to get to know and understand single persons and their needs. More coordination is necessary because this approach is an integral part of the total church ministry. As the ministry grows, it will need some budgetary commitment.

Once the commitment is made and a balanced ministry begun, it will attract single adults willing to give of their time, energy, and resources to make the ministry work. People will respond on the basis of needs and gifts.

Advantages of the balanced ministry include:

- Provides a mechanism for meeting the needs of the total single adult within the church structure

- Can be designed to attract single adults of all ages and types (single, single-again, widowed, divorced, single parents, career-single, single-by-choice)

- Keeps a strong spiritual emphasis while encouraging personal growth

- Reaches single adults for Christ without driving away those who are not yet ready to adopt the Christian lifestyle

- Provides a way for single adults to interact, not only together but also with the entire church family

- Encourages honest, open expressions of personal growth as well as personal failure in the struggles of daily living

- Expresses Christian love and acceptance for people who are often wondering if anyone, even God, actually cares

    The disadvantages of this approach include:
- Requires a great deal of planning, organization, and administration

- Requires a high level of commitment

- Requires an investment of time and other resources

The balanced approach seems the most consistent with scriptural principles about relationships among the people of God and the function of the church.

When God called Moses to lead the Israelites out of Egypt, not only did He provide leadership but also manna, meat, and water to meet their basic needs along the way. When God gave rules about living together in community, He spelled out special instructions for taking care of widows, orphans, strangers, and the poor (see Appendix A).

In the early church, teachers and leaders played important roles. Deacons also were assigned to take care of the daily issues and needs of the people. The apostle Paul says that not to care for our own in very practical ways is to demonstrate that we have not understood the true meaning of Christian faith and community (1 Tim. 5:8).

When evaluating which approach your ministry will take, consider taking the balanced approach even if you want to start slowly. You can have one Bible study a week, one social function a month, one seminar a quarter, one work project a quarter, and one retreat a year for a minimal program.

WHO NEEDS WHOM?

The wonderful truth is: *We need each other.*

Single adults need the church. Some come to church hurting, with a desire to be comforted and healed. Some come to learn to accept singleness. Some need the caring assistance and spiritual reassurance found in a Christian setting. Single adults, healthy in their personal and spiritual lives, still need the fellowship of believers worshiping and serving together. Many need to serve, give, belong, and participate. Single adults need the church.

The church needs single adults. Jesus lived His life on earth as a single adult. There are many single adults in your community who have a lot to offer the church and its ministry. The church needs to hear the perspectives of single adults and benefit from their gifts, abilities, talents, energy, and offerings. The church needs the insights, love, and fellowship of single adults.

Sometimes one of the barriers to developing a single adult ministry that is integrated with the ministry of the church is the traditional prejudice between single and married adults. On both sides of the schism, "we-they" attitudes prevail.

Married adults tend to see single adults as *those people who are not married like we are.* Sometimes married adults feel a little envious of the freedom of choice available to the single individual. They may fear that one's spouse may be attracted to a single adult of the opposite sex or to the free lifestyle. Attempts to play matchmaker involve elaborate schemes to couple single adults so they can achieve marital bliss. Sometimes feelings of superiority exist. Or inferiority. Surprisingly, these perceptions are rarely based on individual comparisons but on generalizations about a married versus single status.

Single adults view married persons as *those people who have no idea (or have forgotten) what it is like to be single as we are.* This attitude fosters withdrawal from, or discounting of, the opinions and suggestions of a married person. Single persons may fear being judged a failure. Sometimes they feel superior, at other times inferior. This attitude is also based on generalized comparisons of status rather than individual realities.

In both cases, the emphasis is on *married* and *single* rather than the common challenges or similar joys.

The winning attitude for a church aiming for a successful single adult ministry is that *we* are all the body of Christ. *We* each have *our* places, *our* functions, and *our* reasons for being. Marital status is only one part of *our* personhoods. *Our* God-given talents and gifts that *we* are to use in the ministry of *our* church have nothing to do with whether or not *we* are married! God does not give one person half of a gift that is useless until the partner who holds the other half is found and married.

We are all the body of Christ. *We* are all the church. *We* need each other.

One of the advantages of integrating relationships within the church is that single and married adults can learn from each other about personal identity and marital relationships. When judgmental and fearful attitudes are changed to acceptance, people begin to draw upon each other's experiences.

People learn from each other what seems to make relationships within a marriage work, as well as what is detrimental to successful relationships. People learn ways to successfully develop a personal identity of wholeness that does not depend on being married or unmarried. They begin to see the tragic results of following worldly values. They can encourage each other as they share the joy of placing Christian values first.

As people share and work together, they express oneness in the body of Christ. One member is not ignoring or rejecting another because of differences. All members recognize that they have an integral part in the ministry needed for the body to be complete. People begin to pull together for the work of Christ. What an exciting vision!

CHECK YOUR REASONS

✔ 1. List the reasons you do not have a single adult ministry. Are your reasons valid?

✔ 2. List the reasons you think you need to develop a single adult ministry. Are your reasons valid?

✔ 3. Outline the type of ministry you would like to develop. In what ways is it like that recommended in this chapter? In what ways would it be different?

If these questions have helped you identify areas in which you could improve your ministry, take action today!

Part II

Begin with the Basics

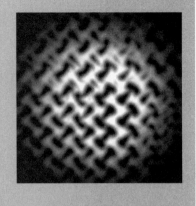

chapter 3

START WITH AN ASSESSMENT

"I have a terrific idea for a single adult center," Carl shared with his pastor one evening. "We could use the church basement and open it up during the week for a gathering place for lonely single adults. It could be fun!"

"How do you know that a single adult center is what we need first?" the pastor asked gently.

"I don't know that we need it first, it just seemed like a great idea," Carl admitted slowly.

When you are ready to take action, begin by assessing, evaluating, researching, and planning. Get a look at the big picture so you can determine just what you want to accomplish and in what order.

Planning is important. Jesus cautions people to carefully count the cost, to lay out a reasonable plan when starting to build so that there is a reasonable expectation that the project will be a success (Luke 14:28–30).

There are several steps to take when assessing the possibilities for a ministry with single adults.

ASSESS YOUR COMMUNITY

As you plan to begin a ministry with single adults, consider the composition of the community where your church is located. This can be done informally by talking with members of your church who live in the area. Get a general "feel" of the community.

You also can canvass the neighborhood by going door to door leaving information about your church and the ministry you hope to begin. If the information has a return card, you may get some responses, giving you an indication of the interest.

You could sit down with the single adults in your church and ask them for input. They may have enough information to give you a good idea of the possibilities for ministry.

For a moderate fee, you can subscribe to a service and obtain a complete analysis of your community by age group, education, career, income level, ethnic breakdown, gender, marital status, and even preferred leisure activities! This will assist you in planning for an effective ministry.

At the very least, discover which churches in your area have ministries with single adults. Visit them. Note the response.

ASSESS THE SINGLE ADULTS IN YOUR CHURCH

If you have access to the right data, you will be able to identify the single adults who are members or regular attendees of your church or Sunday school. This can become the nucleus for your first leadership team. You can use your enrollment data, conduct surveys, or do a mailing to all members of the church asking single adults to respond. You can make an announcement in church or in the bulletin asking that single adults identify themselves. You could also put information cards in the bulletin for several Sundays that single adults can fill out and drop in with the offering.

After you discover who the single adults are in your church, you will want to get their input about needs. Find out what they want in a ministry designed especially for them.

Announce a planning meeting and invite interested single adults to attend. At the first session, discuss the special interests and needs of your own church and community. A small church in Kentucky and a large New York City church would not plan identical programs. The needs of the single adults are different. Let the people who have indicated an interest by attending the meeting assist you in deciding how best to initiate a ministry.

ASSESS YOUR BEGINNING STRATEGY

Your vision for a successful single adult ministry may be grandiose and wonderful. But when you are beginning, keep your plans simple and basic. Set reachable and realistic goals. Develop plans to reach the goals. Do only those things that will help you reach your goals. Without a well-thought-out plan, you will run the risk of wasting time and effort and of getting bogged down with nonessential activities. If you're excited about beginning a ministry, begin with the basics: Bible study, fellowship, small-group discussions, and socials. (Detailed ideas for fully developing each of these are given in subsequent chapters.)

Selecting the leaders for each aspect of ministry; developing bylaws, duty statements, procedures and policies to cover every contingency; and getting involved in outreach, special events, conferences, retreats, concerts, and short-term mission trips need not be included in the first couple months of your new ministry. At a first planning meeting, you might hand out a printed sheet with the following questions:

Bible Study

- Do we want a separate Bible study for single adults?
- When do we want to hold it?
- What topical studies do we want to cover the first month?
- Where will we hold the class?
- When will it start?
- Who will lead it?
- Who will bring the coffee, donuts, cups, napkins, stirrers, creamer, and sugar?
- Who will register and greet the guests?
- How will we publicize the Bible study?

Socials

- How often do we want to plan a social activity?
- What activities do our single adults enjoy most?
- How can we find out which ones they would prefer?
- What will the first four activities be?
- Who will coordinate the first four activities?
- When will we hold the first four activities?
- How will we advertise these socials?

Small-Group Discussions

- What night of the week will we have small-group discussions?
- When should we start small-group discussions?
- Who will serve as discussion leaders?
- What topics should we discuss?
- Who will provide refreshments?
- Who will register and greet guests?
- How will we publicize the discussions?

By answering these basic questions, you will develop an implementation plan for beginning your ministry. The great part of planning as a group is that as people have input into the development of a project, they also feel a certain ownership in the outcome. If your single adults are in on the initial conceptualization of the ministry, they will most likely support it and follow through on their responsibilities.

As you begin, concentrate on the basics. You may have lots of great ideas, but save these for later. After the basic functions are running smoothly, you will have opportunity to refine and improve your single adult ministry.

ASSESS THE SUPPORT OF THE CHURCH

If you are a volunteer or a lay leader within a church that has not had a single adult ministry in the past, or at least the recent past, assess the level of support you can expect from the church.

✔ 1. Meet with your pastor.

The first step is meeting with your pastor. Outline the need for a ministry in your church and discuss your tentative ideas for beginning. Before the meeting, pray that God will prepare the heart of your pastor so there will be a receptivity to your dream and vision. The more detailed and well-thought-out your plan, the more likely it will receive support.

On the other hand, the response you encounter may be more of a "Not now, maybe later"; "Go ahead, but don't expect anything from us"; or a skeptical "I don't think you can pull it off." If you get the approval to begin, consider yourself successful.

If you sense a healthy skepticism but no genuine resistance, then you might continue the discussion by asking your pastor what the signs of a successful ministry would be. For some pastors, success is measured in attendance figures; for others, success is measured by perceived life changes. Whatever the measurement of success, don't forget to keep your pastor informed of the milestones you achieve.

✔ 2. Meet with the church board.

Often the next hurdle is the church board. You may have to make a presentation, a plea, or just an appearance at a board meeting to answer questions. Before you meet, pray that God will prepare the hearts of the individual board members so they will be receptive to your ideas. It is helpful when dealing with a committee or board to have a one-page handout that outlines your proposal and answers basic questions about it. Some people are auditory learners; others are visual learners and need something to look at before making a decision. Be well-prepared, positive, confident but not arrogant, and prayerfully ready to answer questions.

✔ 3. Take the next step.

Whatever the next step is in your church procedures, take it. Sometimes the approving agency is the denominational association or conference. The church council or even the congregation may be the first or last level of clearance. As you plan to initiate a single adult ministry, be sure to follow the established channels to obtain church support. In order to get full support, you will need to be prepared to respond to questions about how this ministry will fit into the overall ministry of the church, how conflicts in scheduling and priorities will be resolved, and the impact a single adult ministry will have on the church.

ASSESS YOUR FINANCES

A successful single adult ministry requires financial support. As you plan your ministry, assess the type and source of your financing. There are several ways to finance a ministry and several ways to keep expenses to a minimum.

Income for your ministry can come from a variety of sources

✔ Allocation in the church budget

Your single adult ministry can be included in the church budget along with each of the other ministries (Sunday school, vacation Bible school, youth ministry, music ministry, missions, etc.). This may not happen the first couple years, but eventually you can hope for this level of support.

✔ Offerings

Collect offerings whenever your group meets formally (Sunday school, small-group discussions, special events, and concerts). These offerings can build a basis for operating your ministry as long as this is consistent with your church policy. If it is policy that all offerings go to the general fund, then discuss the issue with your pastor. Explore ways your single adults can give to support the single adult ministry without violating policy. **NOTE:** Encourage your single adults to continue giving their regular tithes and offerings to the church itself so that the offerings collected for your single adult ministry are above and beyond normal contributions.

✔ Gifts

Some of your single adults (or other church members) may wish to contribute to your single adult ministry by giving cash gifts from time to time.

✔ Fund-raising projects

Many churches encourage special fund-raising projects. These projects are limited only by your imagination and creativity. Examples might include sales of T-shirts or key rings printed with the name of your group; collecting and turning in recyclable materials (paper, aluminum cans, glass); garage sales; bake sales; pancake breakfasts; candy sales; and the sale of entertainment books. Talk with a high school student body coordinator to discover current opportunities for selling products to raise funds.

✔ Pledges

Some groups have augmented their financial base through pledges by group members to contribute a fixed amount each month. **NOTE:** Pledges are honest statements of good intentions. Actual follow-through is much less than 100 percent.

✔ Cost-plus fees

When an event is planned where a fee will be charged to cover the cost of the activity, charge a "cost-plus fee." This fee may be the cost plus five or 10 percent. This small "profit margin" will come in handy if everyone who signed up cannot attend or in the case of an unexpected expenditure. Monies left over after the event go into your single adult treasury.

✔ Token fees

One of the best ways to keep the cash flowing into the group is to charge token participation fees at any get-together where a regular offering is not planned and where there is no basic cost to the group. The fees would never be prohibitive nor would they preclude participation if a person truly could not afford the fee. For example, at an informal party, charge a token fee of $1 per person. (If 20 people attend, that's $20 for the treasury. If there are four parties a month, that's $80 for the treasury.) Most people can afford $1 for a party. Token fees are collected to add to the treasury; the intent is not to pay for the party decorations, refreshments, or room rental.

Expenses

The basic rule of thumb is keep expenses to a minimum without sacrificing the quality of your program and publicity. Show films that only require a freewill offering rather than a large rental fee. Check out a film from the library or borrow a film or video from another single adult ministry in your area. Borrow rather than purchase sports equipment (or have members donate volleyballs, nets, baseballs, bats, etc.). Use facilities and equipment at your local parks and recreation departments. Meet in free clubhouses rather than in rented conference rooms. Some condominium owners or mobile home park residents have free access to their clubhouses for group activities if they make reservations in advance. Hold "last names from A-L bring soft drinks" and "last names from M-Z bring snacks" parties. Plan informal gatherings and potlucks where everyone signs up to bring something. Publicize your group by word of mouth; through free media such as community bulletin boards or announcements on local radio and television stations; post notes on bulletin boards in laundromats and apartment buildings; and of course, alert your church members through your church bulletin and newsletter. Hold "buy-your-own-books" Bible and personal growth studies.

However, you will have some expenses that require a treasury.

✔ Staff salaries

In the beginning, the minister/leader of the single adult ministry may be a lay volunteer. As the ministry grows, however, the church may want to budget for staff salaries for a minister/leader and perhaps a secretary.

✔ Special speakers

Sometimes it is possible to find guest speakers who will donate their time. However, you will usually find that at least a small fee is expected or required. The amount will vary from speaker to speaker and from geographical area to geographical area. If the speaker is from out of town, there also will be transportation and hotel expenses as well as food and incidentals. Ask the speaker up front about these charges, and then determine what your group can afford to pay. If the amounts differ, try to come to acceptable terms.

✔ Scholarship funds

When you can, establish a scholarship fund for single adults who can't afford to attend a special event. Scholarships may be full or partial and may be considered a "loan" to be repaid a little each week. Some people believe that a partial scholarship is better than a full scholarship because the person needs to invest what he or she can. Another way to raise funds for scholarships is to present the need to the entire congregation. For example: "We have 10 single parents who cannot afford to attend the single-parenting conference. Would there be 10 families who would consider sponsoring a single parent by paying the registration fee?"

✔ Emergency-help fund

Some large single adult ministries are able to establish an emergency-help fund for the use of single adults. Such funds are somewhat difficult to manage because each person considers the immediate "emergency" bona fide. The fund may be quickly depleted. Help from this fund can be considered a long-term loan, repayable a little each week.

✔ Working capital

One basic reason for having a treasury is to have the working capital to plan ahead for special events. For example, reserving campsites for a Labor Day weekend retreat may require a 50 percent deposit up to a year in advance. Your single adult group can make such a deposit from the treasury to be repaid later when the cost-plus fees are collected for the event.

✔ Supplies

You may need to purchase supplies if they are not provided by the church or donated by group members. Supplies may include postage and cards for mailings to first-time visitors or ill members as well as Bibles, songbooks, name tags, coffee cups, coffee, creamer, sugar, tea, stirrers, and napkins.

✔ Equipment

When the treasury can afford it, you may choose to purchase some of your own equipment, such as a sound system, folding tables and chairs, and sports equipment.

ASSESS THE REPORTING REQUIREMENTS

Most churches require individual ministries to maintain appropriate records and make periodic reports. Set up a record-keeping system for your ministry. At a minimum, this would include:

Attendance

Keeping track of who attends your ministry activities is not just a "nose counting" function. It is a way of getting to know your members. It's helpful to know who has been absent a couple of weeks and may need follow-up.

Finances

Not only will your ministry be practicing good stewardship, but it will meet accountability requirements if it maintains accurate and comprehensive records of income and expenditures. The system you use must be designed to meet the individual needs of your own group and church. Perhaps you will use a church-owned computer program on a computer owned by one of your members. Investigate whether the church office can maintain the records if there is a staff person who does this for other ministries. Perhaps as your group grows there will be a Certified Public Accountant who will step forward and volunteer to set up an appropriate financial recording and reporting system for your ministry.

Discover what reports will be required of your ministry and set up systems to collect the needed information. Be sure to submit your reports on time. Develop a reputation for punctuality and accountability as well as accuracy.

CHECK YOUR ASSESSMENT

✔ 1. Have you evaluated the community for the potential for a single adult ministry?

✔ 2. Have you identified the single adults in your church?

✔ 3. Have you developed a beginning strategy?

✔ 4. Have you evaluated the level of church support you will receive?

✔ 5. Have you considered how you will finance the ministry?

✔ 6. Are you aware of the reporting and record-keeping requirements needed for your ministry?

If these questions have identified any areas in which you need to do further assessment or research before beginning a single adult ministry, take action today!

chapter 4

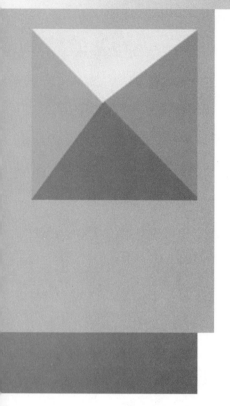

PROVIDE CREATIVE BIBLE STUDY

"I go to church every Sunday. I was raised that way. I believe I should set aside part of my week for God. So I'm not going to change now. But to be honest, something is missing. I don't get as much out of it anymore," Larry stated quietly.

Larry is not alone in his feelings. Many adults believe that attending church and Sunday school is something we do *for God!* They believe they *should* attend faithfully, and they feel guilty if they stay away. The truth is, Bible study is something we do *for ourselves.* As we feed upon the Word, we are strengthened in our spiritual life and become better equipped to meet the challenges of daily living. Our faith is increased as we study the Word of God (Rom. 10:17). Scripture is one of our best defenses against sin (Ps. 119:11). Jesus told us to search the Scriptures because in them we will find eternal life and learn of Him (John 5:39).

Many adults (including those who are single) still remain unmotivated to study God's Word. Some come to Bible study out of habit, others to set a good example for their children, a few come to fellowship with friends, and only a very few come because they are excited about Bible study. There are several things to consider in providing creative Bible study for single adults.

GET PEOPLE INVOLVED

Dave, who was substituting in a large single adult class one Sunday morning, gave the class a real surprise. He announced the topic of the Bible study, posed a few rhetorical but thought-provoking questions, and then read a short passage of Scripture that gave God's principles for action in a certain type of situation. Next, he told the class to work in groups of three or four to apply those principles to a historical case described in an

Old Testament passage that they were to read together.

No one moved. The class was accustomed to a weekly lecture or ser-monette that was always interesting and challenging but required little effort on their part other than listening.

Dave smiled and repeated his instructions. In a couple of minutes, the class came alive. Groups formed in various corners of the room. Individuals opened Bibles and accepted the challenge. Here and there you could hear a friendly argument about exactly how the principles were illustrated in the assigned Scripture reference. Once someone laughed with the joy of discovery. A few people raised their hands to ask Dave clarifying questions. There was a busy hum in the room.

After 15 minutes, Dave asked the people to share what they found. Several spoke at once, then good-naturedly took turns sharing what they had discussed in the small groups.

"Great!" Dave affirmed their efforts. "Now stay in your groups and complete another assignment. I want each person to complete this sentence, 'If I applied the principles we've discussed to my life, I would have to change. ...' Take a few minutes to consider your statements, then share with each other."

This time there was less discussion and a much quieter attitude as people got honest with themselves and with God. For the first time in their lives, some people were seeing things from God's point of view. Those single adults who went out the next week and followed through with those changes had really learned something that morning. When learning occurs, lives change!

Dave knew the secret of effective learning. We learn very little by just listening and observing. We learn most, educators tell us, when we get involved, when we apply and practice what we are trying to learn. Living the Christian life requires specific skills, just as typing, skiing, or playing the piano require special skills. By the Spirit's indwelling power, we grow in these skills day by day.

Involvement-teaching methods can be very simple (circle response, brainstorming, question and answer) or they may be more complicated (producing plays, symposiums, roleplays). Select activities for each session based on the objectives you have set for that Bible study. If you plan your sessions carefully, no two need ever be alike. Your students need never be bored. The following are several Bible learning activities appropriate for adult Sunday school sessions (taken from *Creative Bible Learning for Adults*, Regal 1977).

Discussion

- *Agree-Disagree*—A series of purposely controversial statements on a given subject. Class members indicate whether they agree or disagree with the statements and why.

- *Brainstorming*—Class members suggest as many ideas as possible on a subject, withholding evaluation until all ideas are presented.

- *Buzz Groups*—Small groups (four to eight people) discuss a given topic for a limited period of time.

- *Can of Worms*—Questions or statements on provocative issues are written on separate slips of paper and placed in a container. Groups draw a "worm" from the "can" and respond to it.

- *Case Study*—Real-life problem situations are presented; class members analyze the problems and suggest solutions.

- *Circle Response*—Each person in turn gives a response to a question or statement presented. No one may comment except during his or her turn.

- *Colloquy*—Small-group members present questions about a problem to selected resource persons. The resource persons answer the questions and present additional relevant information.

- *Debate*—Speakers holding opposing views on a controversial subject present their views while the audience observes.

- *Forum*—Open discussion follows a formal presentation such as a debate, interview, lecture, panel, sermon, symposium, etc.

- *Group Response Team*—Several class members interrupt a speaker periodically to request immediate clarification of issues.

- *In-Basket*—Learners are given a situation in which they must respond by setting priorities.

- *Interview*—Learners ask specific questions of a resource person.

- *Listening Teams*—Several small groups, each given specific questions to answer, listen to a presentation and then express their answers to the large group.

- *Neighbor Nudge*—In pairs, class members discuss a given question or subject for a short period of time.

- *Panel*—Several qualified persons discuss a given topic while an audience observes.

- *Picture or Statement Response*—Class members are given a picture (photograph, cartoon, etc.) to look at or a statement to read. Each person gives a sentence response to the picture or statement.

- *Question and Answer*—The teacher guides class members into a given topic or Scripture by asking a variety of specific questions.

- *Screened Speech*—Several small groups devise questions for an expert in a given field. The expert's speech is given in response to the questions.

- *Talkback*—Class members respond to a film, demonstration, lecture, etc., by discussing it in their small groups.

- *Word Association*—Learners are asked to share the first thoughts that come to mind at the mention of a key word.

Writing

- *Abridged Edition*—Individuals or groups read a section of Scripture then condense it to its basic meaning.

- *Acrostic*—Learners use each letter of a key term as the first letter for other words that relate to the key term (e.g., Joy=Jesus, Others, Yourself).

- *Graffiti*—Class members write brief responses to the session topic on a sheet of butcher paper taped to the wall.

- *Group Writing*—A small group of learners work together to complete a writing assignment (story, script, report, etc.).

- *List*—Individuals or groups itemize specific ideas on worksheets or poster paper.

- *Log/Diary/Journal*—Learners gain insights into the feelings and attitudes of biblical characters by writing imaginary entries in their daily logs.

- *Memo*—Class members apply Scripture truths by writing brief memos to themselves summarizing their responses to the lesson.

- *News Story/Headline*—Learners summarize Bible events in headlines or report them in imaginary news stories.

- *Open-Ended Story*—Small groups are given unfinished stories and asked to complete them to resolve the story situation on the basis of scriptural principles.

- *Outline*—Learners list the main points of a Scripture passage in outline form.

- *Parable*—Individuals or groups to write a modern-day parable to illustrate a scriptural truth.

- *Parallel Story*—Learners write a contemporary story to parallel a scriptural event.

- *Paraphrase*—Learners rewrite Scripture verses in their own words.

- *Personalized Verses*—Individuals rewrite key verses using their own names and/or personal pronouns.

- *Poetry*—Several varieties of poetry—rhyming and nonrhyming—may be used to respond to a scriptural truth.

- *Prayer*—Written prayers help learners verbalize their communication with God in more concrete terms.

- *Scrambled Verses or Statements*—Key verses or statements may be scrambled on the chalkboard and teams asked to write them in correct order on worksheets or poster paper.

- *Silent Film Scripting*—Small groups make or view a silent film then write a script that makes the film into a resource for the session objectives.

Art

- *Advertisement Brochure*—Groups design a colorful folder promoting a session concept.

- *Banners*—Letter a key thought or verse from the session on a banner made of shelf paper or butcher paper.

- *Bulletin Boards*—Divide a classroom bulletin board between small groups that decorate each section to correspond with the session theme.

- *Bumper Sticker*—Letter succinct scriptural reminders on strips of paper similar to bumper stickers.

- *Cartoon Strip*—Illustrate a biblical story or contemporary application of a Bible truth in several cartoon frames using simple stick figures.

- *Charts*—Class members graphically display points of information with charts made on poster paper.

- *Coat of Arms*—Individuals illustrate specific aspects of their lives or the life of a Bible character by drawing three or four sections on a shield as a coat of arms.

- *Collage*—An artistic composition is made of various materials such as paper, wood, or cloth glued on a picture surface.

- *Doodles*—Learners respond to a song, story, or lecture by doodling designs or pictures that correspond to what they hear.

- *Frieze*—A series of drawings or pictures tell a chronological or continuing story.

- *Group Drawing*—Class members make a drawing together that expresses a group opinion or discovery.

- *Jeremiah Graph*—Groups read a historical narrative and graph the ups and downs of the Bible characters.

- *Magazine/Newspaper Tear*—Learners tear words and/or pictures from periodicals to represent personal feelings or opinions.

- *Mobile*—Use pictures, shapes, or emblems to create a mobile signifying a scriptural insight.

- *Montage*—Make a composite picture by combining separate pictures.

- *Murals*—Groups work together to create a large painting or drawing on butcher paper depicting a biblical event or practical application of Scripture.

- *Paintings*—Water colors or poster paints are effective media for individuals who wish to paint a realistic or impressionistic scriptural truth.

- *Puppets*—Learners present Bible characters or scriptural characteristics through the use of puppets.

- *Rebus*—Present a Bible verse or session truth by drawing a series of pictures that relate the words phonetically.

- *Slides*—Groups create original slides (photographic, write-on, or ink-transfer) to be presented with live or recorded music or narration.

- *Stained-Glass Picture*—Learners design a meaningful stained-glass window effect by gluing scraps of construction paper or colored cellophane to poster paper.

- *Symbolic Shape*—Learners cut or tear shapes from paper that symbolize a session truth.

- *Time Line*—Class members work together to visualize biblical events chronologically on worksheets or a length of butcher paper on the wall.

- *Word Poster*—Learners cut or tear descriptive words or phrases from magazines or newspapers and glue them on poster paper in a meaningful shape.

Drama

- *Choral Reading*—Groups write and/or read a prepared script in unison.

- *Dramatic Reading*—Learners are assigned different parts of a Scripture narrative or prepared script and read their parts dramatically.

- *Interview*—Bible events come alive when an on-the-spot reporter presents an imaginary interview with biblical characters.

- *Litany*—Leader and group read or recite aloud a script or prayer responsively.

- *Living Sculpture*—Learners interpret scriptural events or concepts by assuming statue-like poses that class members discuss.

- *Movies*—Learners make their own 8mm or video movies outside of class to illustrate a session truth.

- *Pantomime*—Learners act out a situation without speaking.

- *Play Reading*—Class members read a play aloud and then discuss it.

- *Psychodrama*—Individuals act out their own life situations to gain insight into their feelings and behavior patterns.

- *Roleplay*—Learners are given specific problem situations to act out extemporaneously.

- *Skit*—Groups plan and act out a situation that relates to the session.

- *Tableau*—Learners write and present stylized scenes from a biblical story.

- *This Is Your Life*—Class members review the life of a biblical character by presenting imaginary interviews of people who knew him or her.

- *TV Show*—Learners use the format of current television programs to convey session truths.

Music

- *Commercial Jingle*—Groups write new words to the tunes of contemporary commercial jingles to present a message from the session's Scripture focus.

- *Hymn/Song Paraphrase*—Groups rewrite the message of a hymn or song in their own words.

- *Hymn/Song Response*—Learners sing or listen to a hymn or song and tell what it means to them.

- *Hymn/Scripture Comparison*—Groups investigate hymns in the light of their scriptural content.

- *Hymn/Song Rewrite*—Learners write new words that express a biblical concept and set them to a familiar tune.

- *Original Hymns/Songs*—Musically inclined groups can write original music and lyrics based on a session truth.

General

- *Assignment/Project*—Groups complete specific work or study tasks during a class period or at home.

- *Census/Survey*—Learners gather a wide range of personal knowledge and opinion data by asking questions verbally or through written questionnaires.

- *Demonstration*—Individuals demonstrate specific tasks or skills; observers practice what they have seen.

- *Displays/Exhibits*—Individuals examine certain objects or materials that correlate to a session theme.

- *Field Trip*—Learners travel outside the classroom to a location of interest.

- *Games*—Real-life situations are reproduced in a game format so learners can simulate their feelings, responses, etc.

- *Lecture/Monolog/Sermon*—A prepared verbal presentation is given by a qualified individual.

- *Memory*—Class members memorize selected Scripture passages or other related material.

- *Oral Reports*—Individuals share the results of their research with the class.

- *Problem Solving*—Learners are presented a problem to solve that will lead to a better understanding of the session theme.

- *Programmed Learning*—Class members answer questions in a step-by-step fashion with sufficient repetition to ensure learning.

- *Puzzles*—Learners become involved with the session theme by solving puzzles (crossword, word search, scrambled verse or statement, etc.).

- *Recordings*—Learners respond to prerecorded songs, lectures, or dialogs.

- *Research*—Class members practice in-depth personal or group study using the Bible, commentaries, concordance, dictionary, encyclopedia, etc., both in and outside of class.

- *Seminar*—A group convenes for research study under the leadership of an expert.

- *Symposium*—A series of speeches is given by speakers who present selected and related problems.

- *Testing*—Leaders ask for written or oral responses to questions as a means of measuring learning.

- *Visual Aids*—Equipment involves the sense of sight in the teaching/learning process (chalkboard, flipchart, overhead projector, videocassette, filmstrip, chart, map, diagram, work sheet, demonstration, etc.).

- *Workshop*—A group of learners with a common interest meets to explore one or more aspects of a topic.

Use Appropriate Curriculum

"I don't know what to use for curriculum for my single adult class," Sandy admitted to the salesperson at the Christian bookstore. "I know the material we use needs to be relevant, but there doesn't seem to be a lot of curriculum written just for single adults!"

That is true. Some of the curricula currently available is listed in Appendix B, but the list is admittedly short. However, that need not be a major problem. There is no shortage of books with study guides, adult curriculum, or terrific books written specifically for single adults. You have three choices. Use available curricula. Adapt other adult materials, or write your own.

When using either of the last two options, remember that there are four important goals of the lesson plan:

1. Focus the attention on the topic of the session.

2. Get learners involved in exploring the topic and Scripture.

3. Have learners discuss and discover how the principles studied would apply to their lives today.

4. Encourage participants to ask the Holy Spirit's help to make a personal commitment for a life change based on the principles studied.

Remember that even though you want to tailor the sessions to address the needs and interests of single adults, you will want to keep your Bible study focused on the Scriptures. Even if you use a Christian book as the basis for the study, don't forget to keep your single adults involved in looking up relevant passages and seeking answers in God's Word. The topics for your single adult Bible studies need not be limited to divorce, grief, recovery, loneliness, or similar topics. In fact, many of these issues can be better dealt with during week-night support groups because not all the single adults in your ministry will be divorced or grieving the loss of a spouse by death. Plan sessions that address issues from the perspective of those who are single or single again. This is possible even when teaching such "generic" topics as forgiveness, service, the Christian walk, faith development, prayer, stewardship, missions, evangelism, or other aspects of personal and spiritual growth.

Adapting curricula is not as difficult as it may seem. Read through the information provided for teacher background or mini-lecture purposes and change the illustrations to fit the single life and its challenges. You can phrase the assignments in terms of "As a single adult ..." You can personalize the lesson by using illustrations from your own life or stories from the lives of other single adults. When sessions discuss family life, encourage single adults to respond from the perspective of a single parent, a parent without custody, or a "family of one." Once you start adapting curricula, you will develop the necessary skills and will discover that it is relatively easy.

Many leaders of single adult ministries have opted to *write their own curriculum*. If you find a great book that speaks to issues your single adults may be dealing with, or which encourages a deeper Christian walk, you can use it as a basis for your own curriculum. You can provide copies of the book for each of your students, have them purchase their own copies, purchase three to five copies for use in small groups during class, or merely use the book as background material for your mini-lectures.

Design a lesson plan that gets the learners involved in the topic of the day. Start the session with a question, an agree-disagree sheet, a graffiti project, or a neighbor nudge (or any other activity that will quickly get participants to focus on the topic). For a lesson on forgiveness, you might have your single adults turn to one another and share one thing they find hardest to forgive. Suddenly you have them thinking about the topic you will be covering that morning.

Next get the students involved in exploring more in-depth the topic/lesson of the day. This might include Bible research, receiving the background information, or interacting with the main points of the lesson. Many of the methods described earlier will be useful. Don't use the lecture method exclusively. Get students involved in exploring the information for themselves. Divide the class into small groups and give each group a different assignment to prepare and present to the entire class. As they study and prepare their presentations, they will be learning. As the rest of the class listens to the presentations, they will be learning.

Then encourage single adults to apply what they have learned to their own lives and their specific situations. They may return to their small groups to work on an assignment that in some way personalizes the principles covered. If there is time during the session, they may prepare a second presentation for the large group such as a roleplay, poem, song, story, or simply a report of their discussion.

The last part of the lesson plan asks the single adult to make a personal commitment. Often this challenge is an individual assignment. Ask students to pray, write, or respond to one another with a commitment about what they will do with the Holy Spirit's guidance and power during the upcoming week to implement one of the principles considered during the session.

When the time is limited for the session, you may combine the exploration and application segments.

There are a few obstacles to using involvement-learning methods. Some people are uncomfortable at first when asked to do something, to actively participate, in Sunday school. But after a few weeks, most people find the activities less threatening and begin to enjoy themselves. Another problem is that using involvement methods requires more time than simple lecturing. But the rewards and the payoffs in changed attitudes and victorious lives are worth overcoming any obstacle.

FIND AN APPROPRIATE MEETING ROOM

Paul winced as he hit his head on the sloping ceiling of the room where the single adults met. "This place is more like a janitorial closet than a classroom!" he complained.

It's hard for a single adult class to feel very important if they don't have a comfortable place to meet. Of course, sometimes we all have to hold class in an inadequate space. But whenever possible, provide a classroom conducive to fellowship and learning.

Ideally the classroom must be large enough that when the class is subdivided into work teams for an assignment, all of the small groups can meet in the same room. The lighting and ventilation need to be adequate, the room temperature comfortable. Sufficient storage space to keep unnecessary supplies and equipment out of sight and out of the way keeps the room from looking cluttered. Bulletin boards for announcements, chalkboards or flipcharts for illustrations, and projection screens for films, slides, or overhead transparencies add to the functional effectiveness of the room. It's nice to have work tables when they are needed to complete various project assignments.

Perhaps the most important asset you can have in a classroom is chairs that can be easily shifted into various seating arrangements. For large-group activities, a circular seating arrangement is casual yet effective (if the class size is not too large), however theater style is fine for your larger classes. If work teams are planned, the chairs can be set up in small circles around the room.

Single adult groups often meet in various locations besides the traditional Sunday school classroom. Some gather in the meeting room of local restaurants, others in bank conference rooms or community service centers. A few meet in the recreation room of a member's apartment building or at a member's home. One problem with using off-site locations is that the Bible study must be held close enough to the church so it is convenient for members to drop their children off at church before class and to return in time for the worship service.

CHOOSE THE BEST TIME

Although Bible study needs to be a weekly activity, when it is held is up to you. Sunday morning is a favorite time because many people are used to coming to Sunday school, most people don't work on Sundays, and it is a convenient time for parents who bring their children to Sunday school.

Another popular alternative is planning the single adult Bible study for Sunday evenings. This works well in churches with no Sunday evening services. Studies also may be scheduled either before or after Sunday evening services. This allows single adults to attend a mixed adult class on Sunday mornings or to work as a teacher in one of the other departments and still be free to attend their own class for single adults.

Week-night Bible studies draw single adults who can't attend on Sunday mornings and those who wish to study more in-depth than time allows on Sunday morning. Classes may be held during the day, Mondays through Fridays, for those who work nights and weekends. But this alternative needs to be in addition to, not in place of, one of the more traditional times.

When deciding the day and time of your weekly Bible study, be sure to ask your single adults for input. They are the ones who know which times will be best attended.

Take the Challenge

Providing creative Bible study for single adults costs you a lot of time and energy. As singles grow in the grace and knowledge of Christ, it's clear the results are well worth the investment.

Check Your Single Adult Ministry

✔ 1. Do you have a weekly Bible study?

✔ 2. Are the sessions geared to addressing the needs of single and single-again adults?

✔ 3. Are the single adults involved in the learning process?

✔ 4. Do the lesson plans include interest catching, exploring the Word, application, and making a personal commitment?

✔ 5. Are the lesson plans varied each week so that the sessions are different from one another?

✔ 6. Is the classroom the best it can be?

✔ 7. Is the Bible study held at the most appropriate time?

✔ 8. Is the attendance at your Bible studies representative of your entire single adult group?

If the above questions have helped you identify opportunities for improving your program, take action today!

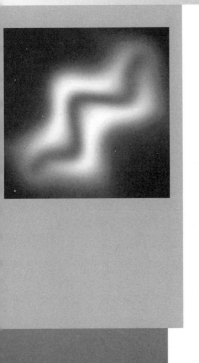

chapter 5

ORGANIZE SMALL-GROUP DISCUSSIONS

"... and there I was, hiding in the bathroom just because Joseph's new wife was with him when he came to pick up the kids," Tammy confessed in a small voice, then laughed sheepishly at herself.

The others in the small-group discussion joined in her laughter, reassuring her that they understood perfectly. A few minutes later, the group mood shifted as another member told about a hurt too recent to be funny. A few wiped away tears as they shared in his pain. As each member opened up to the group, a bond was forged, and each individual felt renewed and strengthened by the caring support of the others.

Most of us want someone to listen to us at times. We want to share our successes, failures, ideas, problems, pain, fun, thoughts, fears, and dreams. We have our own style of sharing. Some of us only share the good things, others only the bad. But most people need someone to talk.

Often single-again adults feel this need more acutely than married adults because either a spouse or companion, an adult-listener role, has been lost.

An important element of a successful ministry is a weekly, small-group, guided discussion. In some cases, these are support groups. They also may draw in the unchurched single adults who have a need for personal contact and affirmation. Successful small-group discussions take careful planning and, when possible, trained leaders for each group. Here are some ideas if you are planning to begin small-group discussions for your single adults.

AN OVERVIEW OF SMALL-GROUP DISCUSSIONS

Because fellowship is important, you may want to provide coffee and doughnuts (tea and cookies or other snacks) before you actually start. You could also complete the evening by adjourning to a nearby restaurant for dessert after the discussion is over and people are feeling comfortable with one another.

You may begin an evening of small-group discussion with music, but this is not required. Keep everyone together as a large group at the beginning of the evening. Give any appropriate announcements, invite participants to attend other functions of your group, particularly the Bible study, provide calendars of your upcoming events, and announce the topic of the evening. In some cases, you may even present a mini-lecture, a skit, a reading, a panel discussion, or some other innovative attention getter that will cause the participants to begin thinking about the evening's topic.

Next, set guidelines for participating in the small groups. Consider the following or develop your own.

1. Everyone will be given an opportunity to share. No one person will be allowed to dominate the discussion.

2. No one will be forced to share. If you don't want to respond to a specific question or statement, you can pass.

3. No one will repeat what is said by others in the small group outside of the group. Confidentiality will be maintained.

4. Each person who shares will do so using "I" statements. Share what you think, feel, and know.

5. No ridiculing. This will be a safe environment to share.

6. The designated group facilitator will be responsible for monitoring the group, ensuring that the discussion stays on target, and that each person is following the guidelines. Participants will cooperate with the facilitator.

Printed discussion guides will be handed out to each group/participant and time given for the discussion. In most cases, it will take a group of 10 people about an hour and a half to respond to seven or eight questions and statements.

Getting single adults into small groups may be accomplished in a variety of ways. The facilitators can come to the front of the room, or stand around the room in the locations of the small groups, and people can select the leader they wish to join. When the group reaches 10 members, it is closed for the evening to allow a reasonable amount of individual sharing.

Some churches prefer to permanently assign members to specific small groups to foster a genuine caring attitude within each group. Visitors and new members may be assigned to existing groups or they may be grouped together to form their own group. The free-choice method is recommended. It's simplest. Also, people who want to can join the same group week after week.

It is important to keep the groups in the same large room if at all possible. As the discussions get involved, the noise level will rise; however, group members will automatically draw closer together to be heard. Being in the same room gives a feeling of togetherness, unity, and excitement.

If someone in a small group demonstrates a need beyond what can be met through the discussion, the facilitator can signal the leader for assistance.

When appropriate, at the signal to close the discussions, the small group participants may join in a closing prayer.

After each session, the facilitators might ask themselves, "If I had been a new person in my group tonight, would I be excited and encouraged to come back next week?" If not, plan to improve facilitating skills.

FIND GOOD LEADERS FOR YOUR SMALL GROUPS

If your single adult group is small, or if you are just beginning and do not have a core group of leaders to facilitate each of the small groups, you can conduct small-group discussions without leaders in each group. It's important to monitor each of the groups to ensure that the guidelines are being followed and that the discussion stays on track.

When selecting facilitators, choose people who know how to listen, who won't dominate the discussion themselves, who won't ridicule, and who are assertive enough to handle difficult or sticky situations. A good facilitator is willing to share personal struggles and experiences and still encourage others to share. Perhaps the best preparation for new leaders is to have them sit in for a few weeks with an experienced and effective facilitator.

Once you have selected small-group leaders (including backups and additional leaders you will need as your group grows), provide training. During the training sessions, help them practice such skills as:

✔ Getting people to open up and share

✔ Keeping the discussion on the subject

✔ Not dominating the discussion

✔ Making sure that everyone understands what is being said by asking clarifying questions or restating what was said

✔ Turning questions back to the group

✔ Asking reflective or summarizing questions

✔ Knowing when to allow someone a little extra time to think before attempting to share

✔ Being honest with the group

✔ Allowing the group to disagree

✔ Allowing a short period of silence

These skills are not learned just by reading a list of "dos" and "don'ts." These skills, like any others (such as skiing, cooking, or swimming), are learned by practicing them over and over again. Use roleplaying, demonstrations, and even videotaping methods to your advantage during the training sessions.

HANDLING SPECIAL SITUATIONS

Successfully leading small-group discussions requires unique skills whenever special situations arise. The discussion leader must take control without creating a hostile or defensive climate for the discussion. Here are some tips for discussion leaders.

• *To call attention to a point that has not been considered:* "Has anyone thought about this phase of the issue?"

• *To question the strength of an argument:* "What reasons do we have for accepting this point of view?"

- *To get back to causes:* "Why do you suppose someone would take this position?"

- *To question the source of information or argument:* "Do you know that as a fact, or is it your opinion?"

- *To suggest that the discussion is wandering from the point:* "Can someone tell me what bearing this has on our problem?" or "Your point is an interesting one, but let's get back to the discussion question."

- *To call attention to the difficulty or complexity of the issue:* "Aren't we beginning to understand why some of us are having difficulty with this problem?"

- *To register steps of agreement (or disagreement):* "Am I correct in assuming that we all agree (or disagree) on this point?"

- *To bring the generalizing speaker down to earth:* "Can you give us a specific example on that point?" or "Your general idea is good, but I wonder if you can illustrate that point from your own experiences?"

- *To handle the impatient, cure-all member:* "But would your plan work in all cases? Who has an idea on that?" or "Hadn't we better reserve judgment until we all know more about this problem?"

- *To suggest that personalities be avoided:* "I wonder what bearing this has on the questions before us?"

- *To suggest that some are talking too much:* "Are there those who haven't spoken who have ideas they would like to present?"

- *To suggest the value of compromise:* "Do you suppose the best course of action lies somewhere between these two points of view?"

- *To suggest that the group may be prejudiced:* "Is our personal interest in this question causing us to overlook the interests of other groups?"

- *To draw the timid but informed member into the discussion:* "Can you share your ideas on this subject with the group?"

- *To handle a question the leader can't answer:* "I don't know. Who does?"

- *To encourage a speaker to talk with the group, not at the leader:* "Don't you think you'll be heard better if you face the rest of the group?"

- *To cut off a speaker who is long-winded:* "While we're on this point, let's hear from some of the others. Can we save your other point until later?"

- *To take the play away from a verbose member:* "You've raised a number of interesting points that should keep us busy for a good while. Would anyone else like to comment on them?"

- *To help the member who has difficulty expressing himself:* "I wonder if what you're saying isn't this ...?" or "Doesn't what you've said tie in with our subject something like this ... ?"

- *To encourage further questions by friendly comment:* "That's a good question. I'm glad you raised it. Anyone have an answer?"

- *To break up a heated argument:* "I think we all know how Tim and Pete feel about this. Now, who else would like to express an opinion?"

- *To assist someone who bursts into tears:* "Sometimes sharing with others can open up hurts. Can someone else share on this topic?" (If the person begins to cry uncontrollably, then signal for a member of the group to offer to take the person to a place where they can talk more privately.)

Not only must your leaders be skilled in small-group dynamics, but you must also have topics that will capture the interest of your members.

CHOOSE INTERESTING AND BENEFICIAL TOPICS

Don't select topics for discussion in a hit-or-miss fashion. Guide sheets should be typed and duplicated well in advance of the session. Have an overall plan for the year or at least for several weeks at a time. Weave the Christian dimension into the fabric of the discussion. Share Christian perspectives. Don't preach.

There are many ways to select appropriate topics for discussion. Get a group of key single adults (or the facilitators for your small-group discussions) together to brainstorm a list of possible topics. Begin by asking such questions as:

- "What challenges do you face most often?"

- "What areas of your Christian walk are you finding difficult at this time?"

- "What are single adults talking about right now?"

Frequently topics include: dating; relationships; single parenting; meeting new people; growing spiritually, emotionally, or personally; anger; love; fear; work; commitment; loneliness; happiness; leadership; communications; goals; lifestyles; changes; hurting; sexuality; and finding a mate.

Perhaps you will want to select key concepts from any number of excellent Christian or personal growth books. Build your own discussion miniseries.

When you have selected the topics, begin developing questions and statements to keep the discussions on target.

DEVELOP DISCUSSION GUIDE SHEETS

Written guide sheets are essential for effective and on-target discussions. If possible, duplicate copies for each participant. If you can't, try to provide one copy for each facilitator. At the very least, make an overhead transparency and project it so that everyone can see the questions from anywhere in the room.

The guide sheets supply the questions (or discussion starters or sentence completions) each facilitator will follow during the discussion. The best type of question or statement is *open ended*. It invites the individual to share. Examples: "The last time I took a risk in a new relationship ... " or "What experiences have you had as a single parent that have made you laugh?" An open-ended question or statement leaves space for a person to be as open as is comfortable. It does not pressure anyone into sharing more than he or she desires at the time.

Other types of discussion-provoking questions get the group members involved in clarifying or summarizing what has been said. Examples: "Peter, would you please summarize what the group has said about prayer?" or "Charlie, how could you say the same concept in another way?"

Avoid questions that can be answered with "yes" or "no." These do not encourage expression of ideas and feelings. Examples: "Do you think you should criticize others?" or "Do you feel afraid in a new relationship?"

Avoid leading questions that clearly indicate the "correct" answer. Examples: "Do you believe a Christian should hold a grudge or forgive others?" or "If you really love your friend, what will you do when he asks to borrow your car?" These questions may encourage discussion, but they do not encourage honesty because the way they are stated indicates the response you want. A better way to approach these topics is to ask questions such as: "What makes forgiving a difficult thing to do?" "When is forgiveness hard?" "Describe a true friend." "What qualities do you value most in a friend?" Writing effective and appropriate questions is not the easiest skill to learn, but it can be perfected with practice.

A natural flow in the discussion guide must be nonthreatening but profitable. At the start of the discussion, members introduce themselves. The opening question is light, fun, and entertaining. A more serious vein can be developed with each succeeding question or statement. Move slowly and carefully. Phrase serious questions to allow varying degrees of openness and honesty. Allow the participants to respond from where they are right at that moment. For example: "I resist God's power in my life when … " can be easily answered by saying " … I yield to temptation." Or someone may be more open and share, " … I rush into a relationship and find myself too involved to ask if this relationship is part of God's will for my life."

The last question is designed to guide members to plan positive choices for the next week. These choices can be a measure of personal growth as, week by week, step by step, individuals show progression as they follow their choices.

The following pages provide sample discussion guide sheets.

CHECK YOUR SMALL-GROUP DISCUSSIONS

After a few weeks of conducting small-group discussions, you will want to evaluate your effectiveness. Here is a checklist you can use.

✔ 1. Do you provide refreshments?

✔ 2. Do you plan your discussions well in advance?

✔ 3. Do you provide written guide sheets?

✔ 4. Are your discussions organized but informal?

✔ 5. Are your discussions lively?

✔ 6. Are visitors made to feel welcome and included?

✔ 7. Is there freedom to express one's self freely?

✔ 8. Do you have enough discussion facilitators?

✔ 9. Are your facilitators trained?

✔ 10. Do your facilitators maintain control in the groups?

✔ 11. Do your facilitators also share in the groups?

If the previous questions have helped you identify opportunities for improving your program, take action today!

Session 1: Social Growth

Read Luke 6:28–31, 37–38

1. Describe the party you would have if you had unlimited wealth and wanted to give "the perfect party."
2. In what ways are cliques beneficial or harmful?
3. Describe the first boy-girl party you attended.
4. How did your first social experiences affect your social growth?
5. In what ways do you grow through rejection experiences?
6. Describe the ways you have grown socially in the last six months.
7. What social skills are you developing at this time?

Session 2: Personal Growth

Read Ps. 1:1–3; Joshua 1:8–9

1. What does "success" mean to you?
2. Describe your biggest success before the age of 10.
3. Tell about someone who has definitely influenced your personal growth in a positive way.
4. Share a struggle you are having in your life and how you are "growing through it."
5. Share some of your long-range goals for personal growth.

Session 3: Family Growth

Read Prov. 17:6, 25; 18:19; 19:26; 20:20; 23:24

1. What was your nickname when you were a child?
2. Whom do you consider your immediate family at this time?
3. Describe the relationship(s) within your family.
4. Share your feelings about where you are in relationship to your family.
5. In what ways do you feel you are either exceeding or not fulfilling your parents' expectations for you?
6. How do outside influences affect your family relationships?
7. How do you share love with your family?
8. Share how you and your family are growing together.

Session 4: Spiritual Growth

Read Eph. 4:11–17; 2 Peter 3:17–18; 1 Cor. 3:6–7; Matt. 13:3–8, 18–23

1. Describe your first experience with prayer.
2. Share your first concepts of God and heaven.
3. When and how did you first become aware that God loves you?
4. Describe an experience you had that helped you grow spiritually.
5. When do you get a "spiritual life"?
6. What goal have you set and are you working toward in the area of spiritual growth?

Session 5: Anger

Read Ps. 4:4; Eph. 4:26; Col. 3:8

1. What things triggered anger in you as a child? as a teenager? as an adult? as a parent?

2. What does your anger look like to others?

3. How can you share your anger in a nondestructive manner?

4. When someone else is angry, what is your response?

5. Share an experience when you were angry and handled the situation effectively.

6. What have you learned through your anger?

Session 6: Being Open and Authentic

Read 2 Cor. 5:10–11

1. When are you least open and authentic?

2. When do others have to listen for what you are *not* saying?

3. What are some ego defenses you use to protect yourself from hurt or anxiety?

4. Describe how you feel and react when your "true self" is about to be revealed.

5. Share about a friend with whom you are not afraid to be "just yourself."

6. Describe how you are becoming more honest and open.

Session 7: The Joy of Giving

Read Matt. 7:9; Luke 6:38

1. What does "giving" mean to you?

2. Describe how you feel when someone gives to you.

3. Describe how you feel when you give to someone.

4. Share an experience when you gave joyfully.

5. Share an experience when you received a totally unexpected and neat gift.

6. If you had unlimited wealth and time, what terrific gift would you give someone special? To whom would you give this gift?

chapter 6

A BALANCED CALENDAR

"I never knew a church group could meet so many of my needs as an individual," Warren commented. *"Just look at this month's calendar. There's weekly Bible study, small-group discussions, a bowling night, parties, special workshops, a support group for single guys, and a retreat next month. I just take my pick of activities and go! In fact, I could do something with the group almost every night."*

What does the calendar for your group look like? Is it full? Is it creative? It can be. Obviously, Warren belongs to a large, active single adult ministry with choices of activities during the month. A smaller church or a group just getting started will have fewer activities.

PLAN TO MEET YOUR MISSION

The activities to include on your monthly calendar are those that meet the objectives of your ministry. Always plan a balanced calendar of events.

Because you will want to provide for *spiritual growth*, include Bible study, worship services, prayer meetings, and workshops. Giving single adults *emotional support* will require small-group discussions, fellowship, counseling, workshops, and seminars as well as support and recovery groups. Encouraging *social interaction* leads to parties, sports, helping-one-another projects, and informal get-togethers. Assisting single adults in *educational development* calls for seminars, retreats, and training sessions. Involving your single adults in *service* means including projects, mission trips, fund raisers, and work days.

Whatever the specific objectives for your single adult ministry, you will need to plan functions appropriate for each of those goals. Don't plan only for Bible study or just for fellowship. Keep your calendar in balance.

Planning Guidelines

"Back in my home church, we used to …," Mike started to explain to the planning committee.

The others looked at each other knowingly and settled back resignedly to listen to another one of Mike's dissertations on how to do outreach. Mike came from a large church with an active single adult ministry and couldn't seem to understand why a small group couldn't operate the same way as a large one.

After Mike finished with a triumphant, "So let's do it that way," the others tried to explain the problems with his idea.

The most important guideline is: Match your program to your single adults, church, and geographic area. Here are some other guidelines.

Check the church's master calendar before finalizing your plans

Don't create scheduling conflicts with the church's master calendar. This doesn't mean that you can't hold simultaneous events, but don't plan to use the church kitchen on the same day another banquet is scheduled. Don't plan to use the gym at the same time as the Junior High Department.

Consider the most appropriate day of the week for events

Some activities are more suited to one day of the week than others. *Sundays* are appropriate for Bible study, worship services, brunch, short afternoon functions (tennis, bowling, picnics), service projects (visiting shut-ins, sick members, or services at a local retirement home, prison, or jail), evening services, "afterglows," and sing-alongs. *Mondays through Thursdays* are good evenings to plan informal get-togethers, special topic seminars, small-group discussions, and service projects. *Fridays and Saturdays* may be date nights for your single adults, but they are also the best times for organized parties and socials. *Saturdays* are perfect for breakfasts, work days, special events (trips to the zoo or theater, one-day conferences, leadership training seminars), and activities that include children as well as adults.

Plan events of interest to your own single adults

Some activities will be of more interest to your single adults than others. Duplicate a questionnaire to distribute to your single adults to determine which activities will be the most successful. You may wish to include the following options on the questionnaire.

Bible-Related Functions

- Sunday morning Bible study
- Sunday morning worship service
- Sunday evening service
- Weekday Bible study (book by book)
- Weekday Bible study (special topics)
- In-depth Bible study (doctrinal issues)
- Bible conference

Sports Activities

- Archery
- Boating
- Bowling

- Bird-watching
- Baseball
- Bicycling
- Camping
- Car races
- Fishing
- Football
- Hiking
- Hunting
- Horseback riding
- Ice-skating
- Jogging
- Racquetball
- Roller-skating
- Running
- Swimming
- Sailing
- Skiing
- Sledding
- Snowshoeing
- Softball
- Tobogganing
- Target-shooting
- Volleyball
- Waterskiing
- Walking

Eating Activities

- Baking party (for holidays)
- Breakfast out
- Barbecue
- Dinner out
- Picnic (beach, park, backyard)
- Progressive dinner
- Potluck dinner
- Taffy pull

Arts and Crafts

- Art show (professional and do-your-own)
- Art gallery visit
- Plays (attending or producing)
- Photography
- Quilting bee
- Sewing party
- Model building

Fellowship

- Amusement park
- Bus or trolley ride
- Circus
- Community recreation program or class
- Drives (to see lights at holidays or flowers in bloom)
- Game night (table games at someone's home)
- Holiday, theme party
- Museum visit
- Music concert
- Play tourist in your own town
- Small-group discussion
- Square dancing
- State or county fair
- Visiting another singles ministry

Service Projects

- Church workday
- Help-each-other workday
- Holding worship services at jails, convalescent hospitals, or missions
- Visiting shut-ins, sick members, or visitors to the group
- Volunteer work in local facilities

Once your single adults have shared their preferences with you, select activities for each month that provide various types of involvement. Include informal as well as highly structured functions. Plan activities that require a lot of active involvement along with more passive ones. Plan some activities "for adults only" as well as some to include children.

Allow for differing interests

Remember that not all of your single adults will like or attend each of your functions. Be sure to plan for a variety of interests and needs. One reason some people may not attend is because they live on a limited budget. For every event you schedule that is somewhat expensive, be sure to offer several inexpensive or free activities. Most groups plan at least a couple of casual potlucks or snacks-and-sodas evenings during the month.

Single parents may stay away from your events because of child care problems. Anticipate and resolve this problem by providing child care during your activities. Hire a sitter with money from the group treasury or from parental contributions, or collect donations at the activity. The single parents might even take turns watching the children for different events.

A third reason for a lack of attendance may be the frequency of your activities. If you have a special function once a quarter, people may forget to come. On the other hand, if you plan something every night of the week and your group is small, you probably won't get a full house for each function. If you are just starting a ministry, try to plan for Sundays and for one or two activities a week (a small-group discussion night and a social activity).

Have a general annual plan

Some things you may want to do once a year, such as hold a conference, go on a group vacation, or take a short-term mission trip. Some activities can come twice a year, such as a retreat, camp-out, or election of officers. You may host workshops or seminars once a quarter. And once a month you will want to schedule planning meetings with your leadership team. Each week, you should plan for Bible study, fellowship, service, and instruction or support. Don't forget to consider the holiday seasons and the needs of your single adults during such times. If you keep your annual plan in mind, you will be more likely to plan a balanced calendar of events.

HOLD MONTHLY PLANNING MEETINGS

Only seven people showed up at the ice-skating rink for the skating party—50 were expected. The group treasury had to pay for the party, and seven people went home wondering who had planned the fiasco.

Sometimes even the best-laid plans go awry. Ensure success for your events by involving your single adults in the calendar planning process. Announce the time and place of the planning meeting and encourage several people to come. If you hold the meeting at least a month before the month you are planning for, you will have time to develop a good calendar. Follow these steps in the meeting:

1. Review the stated mission of your ministry.

2. Review the guidelines in this chapter.

3. Review what your members enjoy doing based on attendance figures from past events and the results of the survey.

4. Review the calendars for the last two months to see which activities have

been scheduled recently. Don't repeat an activity too quickly unless the members insist.

5. Write on a blank calendar sheet your regularly scheduled activities (Bible study, small-group discussions, support-group meetings, planning meetings, services held at the jail, or visitation nights).

6. Consider which new activities would be most appropriate for the upcoming month.

7. Decide which activities to schedule.

8. Make individual assignments to follow up on any items needed (making reservations, calling to obtain fee information, getting directions to locations where events will be held, hosts and hostesses for parties, and sign-up sheets for bringing food).

9. Decide who will be responsible for coordinating each event. (This doesn't always have to be the social chairperson.) Don't assign a responsibility to someone absent from the meeting. First, call that person and obtain permission, otherwise you'll run the risk of an unwilling person not really giving the project a best effort.

10. Discuss how each event will be financed and when child care will be required.

11. Review the calendar you have planned to see if it offers a balanced schedule.

After the meeting, complete the draft by adding in the information gathered by individual assignments. Verify all phone numbers, addresses, and directions. Have the calendar typed (or typeset) and duplicated (or printed). Distribute to all members and visitors.

The more opportunities your single adults have to fellowship and spend time together, the more they will be able to learn from and help each other. And in so doing, they can grow.

CHECK YOUR CALENDAR

✔ 1. Is your mission for your single adult ministry clear and known by your leaders?

✔ 2. Are the activities planned for appropriate times and days?

✔ 3. Are the activities varied?

✔ 4. Is there regular attendance at activities?

✔ 5. Is the calendar balanced?

✔ 6. Is child care provided when necessary?

✔ 7. Are there enough activities? Too many?

✔ 8. Are your single adults involved in calendar planning?

✔ 9. Are calendars duplicated and distributed to all members and visitors?

If the previous questions have helped you identify areas of your ministry that you could improve, take action today!

chapter 7

Develop a Sense of Community

"I was so depressed when I woke up this morning that I almost didn't come to Sunday school," Mary shared with her classmates. "But I feel so loved right now, I'm glad I came."

"We're glad too," Dottie smiled, giving Mary a warm hug.

That morning, Mary needed encouragement and love. A year ago, Mary had been the giver and Dottie the receiver. The giving and receiving extended to each member of the single adult class. Each individual cared for the others; each felt a sense of belonging.

Jesus commanded the church, the community of believers, to actively love one another (John 13:34–35). Such love is a sign to the world that we are disciples of Christ. This sign of love is inclusive of all people, men, women, and children, married or single.

When people feel others care, they begin to internalize the truth that we are each a part of the body of Christ and that when one person is hurting or in need, then the entire body is affected (1 Cor. 12:25–27). Caring includes not only an emotional feeling but also practical action that demonstrates an emotional commitment. Loving and caring for one another involves being able, and willing, to laugh together and weep together (Rom. 12:15).

When one member of the body of Christ has a problem, Christians should respond with care and take the appropriate action to help bear the burden (Gal. 6:2). When the burden is one of loss and pain, God provides comfort, but 2 Corinthians 1:3–5 suggests that God's comfort may be administered through humans who have themselves experienced loss and pain and been comforted by God through others. This theme of receiving something from God to be shared with others is repeated throughout Scripture and forms a basis for a mutuality of ministry within the community of believers.

Church leaders often wish that today's church members shared that wonderful sense of community found in the early church. That wish is not totally unrealistic! A leader of single adults has a unique opportunity to build a feeling of Christian community into the group. Let's see how this works.

According to Abraham Maslow, all people share a hierarchy of needs. He groups these needs into five categories: physical, security, social, psychological, and achievement. We add a sixth category—spiritual. The contention is that one must effectively meet the needs in the order presented. Example: A person who suddenly has no place to live and no money (physical needs) is more interested in a home and a job than in creative expression (achievement).

Each of us moves up the hierarchy as we meet our needs at each level. Any time a major change occurs in our lives, however, our progress is halted, and we descend again to a lower level of need. For example: Sherri lived in a comfortable apartment, had a good job, enjoyed an active social life, had a good self-image, and was pursuing her photography hobby. Then her best friend died in an automobile accident. Sherri's social life suffered an acute loss and became more important to her than photography. Several months later, Sherri had adjusted to a new social network and was once again eagerly shooting pictures.

WHAT ARE THE NEEDS OF SINGLE ADULTS?

Adults who are suddenly single (by divorce or the death of a spouse) usually suffer losses in each area of need. Let's examine each step.

Physical necessities

Possible physical needs include a place to live, food, clothing, transportation, and emergency money. A newly single woman may have to move into a different apartment or home. She may have to go to work or take a second job to support herself and perhaps her children. She may have child care difficulties. She may have transportation problems that may make getting to work, grocery shopping, or church difficult. She may have "fix-it" challenges: How do you fix a stuck door? When do you change the oil in the car? She may become overly tired from the full responsibility for her home and children. And often she will have financial hardships.

A newly single man may have to move into a different apartment or home. He may have to take on a second job to pay alimony or child support. He may have domestic difficulties: coping with washing and mending clothes, cleaning the house, and cooking. He may get overly tired and often will have financial difficulties.

After a period of adjustment, most people learn to overcome these problems and move to a different level of need. Those who don't either remarry quickly or completely withdraw from life in bitterness.

In New Testament times, Dorcas of Joppa was a woman who worked hard at providing for the physical needs of the needy, often the widows (Acts 9:36–42). Some of the members of your single adult ministry may need assistance with physical needs just as people did in the early days of the church.

Security

Possible security needs include belonging to a group, having a steady job, and finding a safe environment in which to interact with others.

Remember when Saul was converted on the road to Damascus? Interacting with the early believers was not automatic. God had to lead Ananias to Saul and tell Ananias that it was safe to bring Saul into the fellowship (Acts 9:13–20).

Adults who are newly single-again may no longer feel comfortable with the previous circle of married friends or in a couples' Sunday school class. They may feel they have failed to live up to the ideal that "marriage is forever." They may feel they are less acceptable, and they become vulnerable to attack and to criticism. They may not know of a safe place to go to be with other Christians. However, when their security needs are satisfied, they are ready to move to the next level of need.

Social status

Jesus talked a lot about relationships. In fact, He told the disciples that He was giving them a new commandment, that they love one another. This love would be the mark of a true disciple of Christ (John 13:34–35). We all have needs for loving and being loved.

Possible social needs include fellowship, sharing, conversation, working with others, helping others, loving and being loved, accepting others and being accepted, and sharing feelings with others.

People are social beings. We really do need each other. Deprived of social interactions, few people can maintain a healthy psychological balance. We need opportunities to share discoveries, exchange ideas, help others, receive support, laugh together, love, and receive affirmation. In short, *we need to belong*. A supportive social structure is one of our most basic needs. In fact, only when we have a satisfactory social life are we really in a position to develop our self-esteem and meet our psychological needs.

We all define our social needs in different ways. Some of us are happy if we have a few, very close, intimate friends. Others crave dozens of casual relationships. To some, a social life consists of always "doing" something: sports, picnics, or traveling. To others, a party is having a few friends over for coffee and talking.

Developing lasting, close friendships takes a special set of skills, and people who go from one short-lived relationship to another have not learned these skills. We need to always be learning to reach out in love and to care for each other.

Christian social relationships have the added dimension of the spiritual fellowship of 1 John 1:7. Not only are we sharing together, but we also are sharing with Christ.

Divorced or widowed persons need to replace the lost social fulfillment of the marriage with fellowship and sharing with others. When you've finished your evening tasks and had your bath, with whom do you talk? You can telephone a friend, but first you need to have a friend! Who laughs at the little jokes when you're alone? Single adults need to be involved with other adults in special projects, ministry, social settings, and friendships. They need to be accepted and to have their self-confidence restored.

Because adults who are single again have been coupled socially with other adults, they must now establish a new social identity. The circle of friends will change as they reach out to other single adults instead of socializing exclusively with couples. During this period of augmented social need, single adults often want a more active social life. As married couples, people may have been satisfied to go out once a week. Now, as single adults, people may want to go out four or five nights each week.

Included in the area of social needs are sexual needs that range from being touched, held, cuddled, warmed, comforted, and caressed, to being stimulated and fully satisfied sexually. The suddenly single adult is, as one doctor put it, sexually marooned! How do you go from an active sexual life within a marriage to a forced celibacy without problems? You don't! To ignore sexual frustration is to increase the problem, so the single-again *and* the single adult need to openly and honestly discuss this area of need.

The sexual drive God built into every man and woman is an intense force that is not easily deterred or sublimated. It is not enough to tell people they should not give into their urges unless they are living within the sanction of marriage! It takes life commitment to Christ to be able to withstand temptation. People who have just been through the trauma of a divorce or the death of a spouse are usually upset and often have a strong, insatiable craving for attention and affection. To compound the problem, the sex drive and desires influence and interact with a person's entire physical and mental well-being. Single adult ministries need to teach God's ideals for chastity and sexual obedience while openly acknowledging temptations in this area.

Self-respect (self-esteem or psychological needs)

When God told Moses to go to Pharaoh and lead the Israelites out of Egypt, Moses' first response was "Not me! I can't do that!" (Ex. 3:1–4:13). Often the response of adults who are suddenly single is "I can't do this! I can't make it alone!" Their self-esteem is shattered.

Possible self-respect needs include knowing and understanding concepts, receiving and giving affirmation, attention, respect, courtesy, acceptance, understanding, and a realignment of one's personal integrity and identity.

The task of developing a positive self-image is one we inherit half done. Our self-images are built from birth, from bits and pieces of praise and criticism and from successes and failures. Then one day, we take a long, hard look at ourselves and ask, "Who am I?" This usually happens during adolescence. Sometimes we like what we see. Sometimes we don't. Then we begin to make changes so that we can like ourselves. However, the changes that are lasting and do improve our self-image are not those we make ourselves but those God makes in us, as our lives are transformed by the renewing of the Holy Spirit (Rom. 12:1–2; Titus 3:5).

Developing a positive self-image is not a one-time task! It is an ongoing process that takes a lifetime. In fact, during periods of crisis, such as getting divorced or losing one's spouse through death, we often tend to begin doubting ourselves and lose our confidence to be effective in relationships or in any of life's endeavors.

Because single-again adults may not totally accept their new unmarried status, they may project this self-rejection onto others. They may become defensive and hostile, placing out-of-proportion value on an insignificant comment or action.

Sometimes single persons struggle to discover a personal identity. No matter how much a person may have wished to escape a negative marriage or relationship, at least a part of one's own self-image includes the relationship with a former significant other. Now, suddenly alone, single-again adults need to reevaluate themselves and their self-concept.

People whose marriages have ended may consider themselves failures and allow that perception to color the rest of their lives. They may question proven abilities on the job, in social relationships, or spiritual services. The single-again adult needs a group of people who understand because of their own past experience making the transition from half-a-couple to head-of-a-household. When reassured through understanding, praise, courtesy, respect, and most of all belonging, individuals begin to accept themselves and move into another area of need fulfillment.

Achievement

Sometimes achievement means doing the impossible, success on the job, or writing a book. Sometimes it means winning. Sometimes it means just hanging in through tough times. The apostle Paul wrote at the end of his career, "I have fought the good fight, I have finished the race, I have kept the faith" (2 Tim. 4:7).

Possible achievement needs include using talents or spiritual gifts, conquering a challenge, growing as a person, overcoming personal problems (depression, shyness, fear, financial binds), and trying to succeed at something new.

Achievement needs are vital to every human because they symbolize the maturing growth of the individual who has had other needs satisfied and is now ready to express creativity and ability. Because this need does not seem critical until the other needs are met, single adults who reach this step have usually adjusted to the status of being single or single-again. They are ready to reach out and help other adults through their problems.

Single adults at this level of need may be good candidates for leadership in ministry. Leadership can be an outlet for achievement. Responsibilities for projects, socials, teaching a class, or serving as an outreach leader are possibilities.

Spiritual growth

We never outlive our need for spiritual growth. Even though God's ideal for us is to be conformed to the image of Jesus Christ (Rom. 8:29), it is clear we are continually in process while on this earth. Therefore, we look for ways to continually grow spiritually.

Spiritual needs include a wide range of needs from learning to trust God for one's salvation to being fully equipped to do good work through the Holy Spirit. In ministering with single adults in the areas of their other needs, we must not forget to include a significant focus and emphasis on ministering to their spiritual needs.

MEETING THE NEEDS

The involvement of the church in assisting single adults to meet their needs includes taking a close look at the structure, procedures, and policies of the church.

1. Are single adults made to feel welcome?

2. Are they not only allowed but encouraged to serve on committees and boards; as deacons, trustees, and teachers; or on the staff?

3. Are sermons balanced to address the interests of and provide illustrations applicable to couples as well as single adults?

4. What about church functions. Is there still a Sweethearts' Banquet in February or Father-Son and Mother-Daughter events? On Mothers' Day and Fathers' Day, are single parents included and honored? Are tickets discounted for couples or families?

5. Check the church calendar. Are single adult functions included? Do they "bid" for prime dates and times, or do they get only leftovers?

6. Does the church library have books applicable for single adults and single parents?

7. Is child care provided for all functions?

8. What's the first impression of your ministry? Does it appear organized? Is structure effective without being restrictive? Is the room set up appropriately? Does it communicate a sense of pride and welcome? Are there greeters? Are name tags provided? (Yes, I hate them too, but I'll admit, it helps bridge awkward moments if you can see what someone's name is.) Are refreshments provided?

9. Do you provide information on your ministry? (At least a calendar of events, a purpose statement, and telephone numbers of leaders.)

10. What follow-up is there for visitors, those who become ill, or who "fall through the cracks"? Do you have a system to identify and recognize visitors? Is someone assigned to contact them within a week? Who cares for those who turn up "missing"?

The key to building a sense of community within a group is involving group members in meeting the needs of others. As we give to others and assist them in meeting their needs, we build a part of ourselves into the life of the other person. People who are newly single-again need help with physical and security needs, but they can find ways to meet their own social, self-esteem, achievement, and spiritual needs.

Meeting physical needs

Your single adults can help each other meet their physical needs by:

• Opening homes to others who need a place to stay for two or three nights for any number of *temporary* reasons, such as being new in town, just moving out on one's own, or coming to town for a single adult conference.

• Renting a spare bedroom to a single adult on a limited budget

- Assisting in locating a new home or apartment

- Scheduling help-each-other workdays to paint a home, complete major yard work, do minor carpentry, or make plumbing repairs

- Maintaining a special-emergency help fund for single adults in genuine emergencies. (Manage this fund carefully. Encourage single adults to repay the fund as soon as they are able so that others can use the fund. Replenish the fund through donations, special offerings, repayments, church budget allocations, and income from special activities such as garage sales, bake sales, or aluminum can recycling.)

- Providing transportation to church and special events by car pooling or special driving assignments

- Providing opportunities to share food with each other

Meeting security needs

Your single adults can share in meeting these needs by:
- Sharing knowledge of available job opportunities

- Hiring group members rather than outsiders to do jobs whenever possible

- Working with an employment agency to get free job referrals if possible

- Providing free (or inexpensive) child care for working single parents

- Starting a child care co-op for single parents during working hours or when social functions are planned

- Setting ground rules for accepting people where they are in their personal and spiritual growth. (You just care for them. Let God change their lives!)

- Making your ministry a safe place for people to come, be real, and share

- Encouraging members to refrain from criticism, backbiting, gossip, and strife

Meeting social needs

Your members can love by:
- Openly affirming one another

- Giving honest compliments

- Affectionately hugging each other

- Spending time with each other

- Ensuring that everyone feels welcome and no one is ostracized or ignored

- Fellowshiping together

- Developing a sense of belonging within the group

- Including visitors in ongoing events and activities

Meeting self-respect needs

Help your single adults develop self-respect by:
- Giving affirmation, encouragement, and loving support to your single parents

(with Big Brother/Sister-type programs, family activities, child care arrangements, special seminars)

- Giving affirmation and loving support to each person during difficult times
- Rejoicing in one another's successes
- Providing peer (and sometimes professional) counseling as required
- Starting a telephone counseling service
- Conducting small-group discussions
- Involving people in ministry using their talents and abilities
- Publicly giving certificates of appreciation and accomplishments
- Asking for (and listening to) input and advice
- Giving responsibility to individuals

Meeting achievement needs

As your single adults feel secure and loved, they will look for ways to stretch and use their God-given spiritual gifts and their creative talents. Provide for meeting this need by:

- Letting single adults exercise their gifts of leadership, music, art, mechanical aptitude, public speaking, organizing, and helping as they are active in the ministry
- Drawing upon the ideas of your single adults for improving or expanding the ministry
- Providing "personal growth" seminars and workshops
- Hosting conferences for single adults not only from your group but also other churches in the area

Meeting spiritual needs

Make your group a place where people come to grow spiritually by:

- Providing sound biblical instruction
- Providing scripturally based counseling
- Providing opportunities to worship God
- Encouraging single adults to use their spiritual gifts

SPECIAL WAYS TO CARE

How would a visitor describe the caring level in your single adult ministry? Caring and sharing opportunities are an important part of the program. Several church leaders have discovered special ways to care. Here are a few.

Caring units

Small groups are a part of any church. Within the church, people who have a more in-depth friendship together than they do with the entire community of faith tend to group together. Such grouping occurs naturally. However, many churches have deliberately incorporated an organized small-group ministry program within the church. This helps members relate to one another on a more intimate level. A few churches have made the distinction that they do not *have small groups*, but that they *are small groups*.

Small groups can be varied. They may be support groups (AA, NA, ACA, Divorce Recovery, Grief Recovery, etc.); they may be interest groups (cooking, sewing, car restorations, drama, travel, etc.); they may be home study groups in which Bible study or the study of a Christian book is the focus; they may be fellowship and care groups who meet to get to know one another and to invest in the lives of one another.

Whatever the stated emphasis, the underlying purpose is to care for one another. The small-group leader and other members care for each other by keeping in contact through telephone calls, meetings, visits, cards, and letters. Members who are sick or who need special assistance can turn first to the others in their small group, knowing that they will understand their need and most likely respond quickly. Members have an opportunity to use their spiritual gifts as they minister to one another, living out the gospel of Christian love and bearing one another's burdens.

The function of the small group is to care for one another, to develop a close bond of Christian love and fellowship, to minister to one another, and to build the body of Christ into a genuine, caring unit. At whatever level your church may participate in the small-group process, the question is how single adults can be cared for along with married adults.

Different churches include single adults in various ways. Some provide small groups that are strictly for single adults and others for only married couples. This structure appears to be a bit restrictive if groups are assigned without choice. Some single adults will be comfortable in a small group with only single adults, others can function well in a mixed group. Carefully consider these differences in single adults.

Centers for single adults

Depending on available resources, some churches have centers for single adults that are open each night of the week and all day on weekends and holidays. Each center is organized differently, but they all have a common purpose, providing a place for single adults to come and share together. Activities range from table games to volleyball, from Bible studies to potluck suppers, from a place to come and quietly read a book with other people around to a place to come and find someone with whom to talk.

A variation of the center is the concept of a single-adult or single-parent apartment building. These may be owned by the church or jointly by the single adults. They provide low-cost housing, child care co-ops, discounts on food products through bulk purchasing as well as shared recreational and learning activities.

One large church was able to buy an entire block of small, older homes at unbelievably low cost. Church members (including the single adults) worked together to repair and paint the houses and to clean up the yards. As each house was finished, a local bank provided a low-interest loan to a single-parent family from the church. The family purchased the house well below the market rate but at a price that enabled the church to replenish funds and buy additional homes. What a wonderful project!

Help-each-other workdays

"Wake up, Stan! It's Saturday!" Loud pounding on the door emphasized Don's point. Sleeping was out of the question, Stan admitted to himself as he grumbled toward the door.

"Hold your horses, I'm coming," he growled.

Thirty minutes and two cups of coffee later, Don and Stan and their tool-boxes were on their way to Pam's house. Saturday was "fix-it" day. Every Saturday, the single guys get together to do heavy-duty work or odd-job repairs at the single women's houses. Meanwhile, the women prepare a home-cooked dinner for the men. Or the women go to a man's home and do yard work while he prepares the evening meal.

Helping each other is one way to grow and in the process bond together. Car repairs, yard work, moving, painting, cleaning a garage, carpentry, and mending are all ways that single adults can assist one another. But the ways are unlimited.

Single adult telephone line

A staff secretary of a single adult ministry links new people who call in with other single adults. This may include giving out activity information from the calendar of events, giving out telephone numbers of certain members, or making referrals to various support groups. Even if there is not a paid staff person in charge of your single adult ministry, you will want to ensure that this function is handled by someone.

Make copies of your single adult ministry calendar available for the church receptionist or secretary. The calendar provides information for a quick response to a what-when-where question. You also can mail calendars to inquirers. Perhaps one or more of your lay leaders would be willing to have their personal telephone numbers given out to those who call the church. Consider setting up a special telephone number with a recorded message about key events and request a telephone number for a return call.

Because single adults who are newly single-again often need to talk to others who have been through a similar experience, some large single adult ministries have begun a single adult "hotline." Single adults sign up for blocks of time when they come to the church and answer the telephone, talk with callers, provide peer counseling, and pray with them. Such volunteers should be trained as telephone counselors. They need to recognize when a caller needs to be referred to a professional psychologist or minister for additional assistance.

Information

Julie's divorce had just become final, and she realized that she had to get on with her life without hanging onto the hope that the divorce would turn out to be a horrible nightmare. She had heard that her church sponsored divorce recovery support groups and decided she needed to join one of them. Resolutely, she dialed the church office only to be told that the next support group would be held in the fall and that they would take her name and let her know when the sessions were scheduled.

"That's months away. What do I do in the meantime?" Julie asked the telephone as she hung it up.

If your church doesn't provide a particular service, program, or group, find out what alternatives are available in your community. It is unrealistic to expect a hurting person to wait several weeks or months for your next scheduled event. Churches can work together on scheduling events and groups so that whenever a person calls, information or assistance is available right away. At a minimum, provide printed material. (For example: *Life After Divorce*, CPH 1994. Make it available at cost to those who call in asking for assistance coping with a divorce.) Stock the church library with several copies of books on a variety of common topics. You could work with a local Christian bookstore to maintain an adequate stock of helpful books that will be recommended by the church.

Counseling services

Peer counseling is a valuable service provided by various single adult ministries. Volunteers are given basic training in listening, accepting, and recognizing the signs of the seriously troubled. Those who require professional assistance are referred to Christian counselors who provide their time on the basis of the single adult's ability to pay. Larger churches allow pastoral staff time to provide counseling or hire full- or part-time pastoral counselors.

MAKE YOUR MINISTRY UNIQUE

Some of the special ideas presented in this chapter will be appropriate for your program, others will not. Develop your ministry so it is specifically planned to meet the needs of your single adults.

CHECK THE SENSE OF COMMUNITY

✔ 1. Do your leaders understand the hierarchy of human needs?

✔ 2. Is there a plan to assist single adults to:
Meet their physical needs?
Meet their security needs?
Meet their social needs?
Meet their self-respect needs?
Meet their achievement needs?
Meet their spiritual needs?

✔ 3. Are there provisions for caring in special ways?

✔ 4. Is your ministry tailored to your own single adults and their circumstances and perceived needs?

If the previous questions have helped you identify opportunities to improve your program, take action today!

chapter 8

INCLUDE WORSHIP AND MUSIC

I entered the large conference room for the opening general session of the annual consortium of the Network of Single Adult Leaders. The noise was deafening as colleagues greeted each other fondly, sometimes yelling across the room to a late arrival. But as people became aware of the sound of the piano, attention was focused toward the front of the room, and the side chatter ceased as Dennis Franck began leading us in a period of praise and worship. We sang about the Lord. We sang to the Lord. And soon there was a sweet spirit in the room, a oneness, an uplifting, refreshing, awesome combination of peace and freedom that only comes from entering into praise and worship of the King of Kings.

We had come together into the room. But we joined together as we worshiped.

THE PURPOSE OF PRAISE AND WORSHIP

Ed Reed differentiates these terms by saying that *praise* is saying/singing *about* God while *worship* is saying/singing the praises *to* the Lord our God. Thus, singing "God is so good" is praise; singing "You are so good" is worship. Inherent in both concepts is our witness to one another through word and music inspired by our good God.

There is another way of looking at these terms. Praising God acknowledges His attributes, tells about His faithfulness, affirms His promises. It is a conscious affirmation of the Lord. Worship combines the cognitive assent of greatness and adds the emotional and behavioral component. To worship someone, one must give deference, preeminence, and reverence. One acknowledges the superiority of God and in the process humbly asks with David, "What [am I] that you are mindful of [me]?" (Ps. 8:4).

There are song leaders, and there are song leaders. Some people stand in front of a group, announce which song will be sung, and lead the group as they sing. After a few songs, the song leader turns the program over to the person in charge of the next segment. The participants may have enjoyed the music but may not have benefited from it in any particular way.

Other song leaders carefully plan that part of the service or program devoted to music so that the songs tie into the theme. They energetically lead the songs and get people involved. People become generally energized, alert, and ready to participate in the rest of the program/service.

But I believe that true worship leaders are more than people who have the technical skills to plan music. They celebrate their relationship with the Lord and bring the group to a point where the body of Christ is united, communicating with the Lord, and ready to receive what the Scripture will say and the Holy Spirit will apply in their lives.

Music in a single adult ministry may serve various purposes. Playing music as people arrive in a classroom or meeting room can make the atmosphere warm and friendly. Singing boisterous and playful songs can be entertaining and fun. Singing and clapping to rhythmic songs can be energizing, entertaining, bonding for the group, and a way to break the ice. Singing hymns can be a way of exhorting one another, reminding us of spiritual truths. Singing together is a way of bonding, of sharing a spiritual activity. It helps us turn our eyes and hearts to the Lord. Singing praises of God is a way of telling each other what we know about God. Singing strengthens our faith as the Holy Spirit reminds us how great the Lord truly is.

PRAISE AND WORSHIP ARE SCRIPTURAL

Singing praises and worshiping the Lord in song is definitely scriptural. The Bible tells us to sing praises to the Lord (cf. Ps. 47:6–7; 68:4; 75:9; 92:4). In case we can't carry a tune very well, we are even told it is proper to just make a joyful noise to the Lord! (Ps. 66:1; 81:1; 95:1–2; 98:4; 100:1) Various instruments enhance the praises we sing (Ps. 98:6; 144:9; 149:3).

When there were special events in the history of the Israelites, people often would sing about them. Deborah, the prophetess and fourth judge of Israel, and Barak, the sixth judge, for example, sang a song of victory when God delivered them from Jabin, the king of Canaan (Judg. 5:1–31). Hannah prayed/sang when she brought the child, Samuel, to Eli (1 Sam. 2:1–10). Even Mary, the future mother of Jesus, sang/spoke the Magnificat when blessed by Elizabeth (Luke 1:46–55).

When the Israelites returned to rebuild the city of Jerusalem, they gathered together to hear the reading of the Law. It had been a long time since they had gathered for this purpose. As Ezra read, they wept in response. They were convicted and grieved. And Ezra kept reading. They confessed and then *worshiped* the Lord (Neh. 8:1–9:3).

PRAISE IS POWERFUL

Remember the effectiveness of the praises sung by Paul and Silas in prison (Acts 16:25–34)? At midnight, they prayed and were singing, and all of the other prisoners heard them. What a surprising response to being in prison! Perhaps the other prisoners were curious. When the earthquake occurred, instead of running off, the prisoners gathered around Paul and Silas. When Christian martyrs John and Betty Stam were buried alive, they stood with the others in a ditch. As the dirt was thrown upon them, they sang "My Jesus, I Love Thee" until they could no longer sing. What a powerful testimony. God gave them strength to die with dignity as they praised Him.

For your single adults, some of whom may be suffering from a deep grief over the loss of a spouse or from the pain of a divorce, praise and worship can be a powerful way of caring for them. You are helping them experience God's presence in a way that allows them to feel God's healing touch. Many times I have seen single adults weeping silently during worship; often I am overwhelmed myself and find tears rolling down my cheeks as the Holy Spirit opens my heart to God through worship. People who cannot be reached or comforted by words, or by a friendly hug, may be ministered to in praise and worship.

Paul encouraged the early Christians to use singing and music in a purposeful way in their ministries. In Col. 3:16 he wrote, "Let the word of Christ dwell in you richly as you teach and admonish one another with all wisdom, and as you sing psalms, hymns and spiritual songs with gratitude in your hearts to God." And in Eph. 5:19 he wrote, "Speak to one another with psalms, hymns and spiritual songs. Sing and make music in your heart to the Lord."

CHECK YOUR MUSIC MINISTRY

✔ 1. Is the music portion of your ministry effective?

✔ 2. Is (Are) the music leader(s) effective?

✔ 3. Is the music planned to encourage praise and worship?

✔ 4. Does the music help members focus on the session?

✔ 5. Does the music provide an atmosphere of worship?

If the previous questions have identified areas in which you could improve your ministry, take action today!

chapter 9

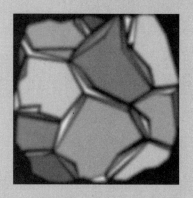

PUBLICIZE YOUR MINISTRY

Ken, Scott, Bill, and Linda, all leaders of single adult ministries in a large city, were having lunch together, discussing ideas for ministry and outreach.

"We had this terrific seminar last month, and only 10 people showed up," Ken complained. *"I don't know what went wrong. The speaker was well-known, the event was well-publicized, and several people told me they would be there and never came."*

"It's frustrating at times," Linda agreed. *"We've had an active ministry for two years now, and it seems we still run about 30 people. It's not always the same 30, but the numbers stay about the same from week to week."*

Single adult ministry in the church is markedly transitional. Single adults come and go, drifting in and out depending on the program, their relationships, their needs, and many other factors.

Single adults go where other single adults are. The larger your attendance, the more apt you are to see the numbers increase. Yet in most ministries, there remains a faithful core group of people you can count on. This core group helps the ministry grow by continuing to reach out to single adults in your community.

SPREAD THE WORD

Even the most elaborate single adult ministry will be a failure if no one attends the planned functions! One of your first steps is to spread the word about your ministry. Let people know where you are and what you plan to do. Of course information sharing is not a one-time activity, it must be an ongoing process using a variety of methods.

The community in which your church is located includes single adults who feel unwanted, unloved, and unnoticed. Share God's love as you show that you notice, that you care. Be creative! Use not only the following approaches but also any great new ideas your group can invent. *The purpose of reaching out is not to increase the number of members in your single adult ministry but to increase the number of people to whom you are ministering.*

Develop a brochure, flyer, or card

Distribute a brochure explaining your single adult ministry to prospective members, visitors, and inquirers. Start with an inexpensive business card giving the title of your group, a name and telephone number to call for information, and the times of your regular meetings.

Another inexpensive handout is a one-page flyer printed on brightly colored paper. As soon as possible, prepare an informative brochure that gives the purpose of your ministry and as much information as possible to attract single adults to come and visit.

Whatever type of card, flyer, or brochure you develop, make it attractive and high quality. This piece of paper will advertise your ministry and will give the first impression of your group. Don't give the wrong message by using a poor quality product with misspelled words or crooked printing.

Use your church bulletin/mailer

Don't forget to routinely announce your program and activities in the church bulletin, mid-week mailer, or newsletter. At least a couple times a year, include a copy of your brochure in the church bulletin. Keep people informed and aware of your ministry.

Knock on doors

In these days of locked apartment buildings and suspicious tenants, you may not get very far knocking on doors. But don't overlook the possibility that right in your church area you can find single adults who would come to your church if they knew about your ministry. One church mailed brochures describing their program to occupants of the apartment buildings in their community. This brought in several new members.

Advertise in the media

Many single adult ministries use the local newspapers to advertise their functions. Some groups run ads in the personals section, others on the church news page. It is sometimes possible to obtain free advertising for major events such as concerts and conferences through public service announcements or community activity notices.

Use your enrollment and church records

Many of the youth and children who attend your Sunday school come from single-parent families. Consider sending home copies of your brochure with these children and young people. Mail literature to those members of your group or visitors to your ministry who have not attended for some time.

Form special interest clubs

One director of a single adult ministry shared his success with forming special interest clubs for such activities as skiing, hiking, sailing, and bicycling. Those members of the group with specific interests planned and coordinated their own activities. Then they invited other single adult friends who were not necessarily interested in church. As these friends became active in the club, many began to attend other functions of the group, even the weekly Bible study.

Plan bring-a-friend activities

The most successful advertising is word of mouth. When your single adult ministry is exciting and meeting the needs of single adults, those who come will want to tell their friends and bring them to share in the ministry. Just as Andrew got excited and brought people to Jesus, your single adults will effectively reach out and draw others into your ministry if they get excited about what you are doing.

Encourage your members to invite their single adult friends to your activities. An invitation "to church" can sometimes frighten away a prospective member, but an invitation to a camp-out or a party is nonthreatening.

One group went camping for a weekend. A guest who attended was a nonbeliever, and he honestly challenged every Bible study, prayer, or discussion. The theme was Christian Love (which he had hoped meant something a bit more physical). Puzzled, he kept watching the men and women sharing, praying, laughing, teasing, and singing. At the sunrise sharing service, which was held on the beach, each person was asked to walk around and find an object to give to someone he or she loved in Christ.

A man found a book of matches. "God loves you; keep the light burning," he said, giving someone a match.

A woman picked up a rock. "God loves you," she shared. "Christ is our rock. Hang on tightly."

The nonbeliever, shocked at being given a flower as evidence of Christian love from a woman who had refused his amorous advances, stammered, "I think I'm beginning to see what you mean by Christian love. This is real!"

Be innovative

The best way to plan your outreach program is to sit down with your single adults and brainstorm all the possible ways to reach others. Remember when brainstorming not to evaluate any idea, just write down whatever is suggested. The craziest comment might trigger the most creative and successful approach on the list.

After you have developed a list of possible approaches, start discussing, evaluating, and combining ideas until you have conceived a viable plan. Your plan must be specifically suited for your own group, geographic location, and program objectives.

Once you have a plan, get started, and don't give up if you meet with some initial setbacks.

PROVIDE WARMTH AND ACCEPTANCE

Alan's life was shattered into a million pieces, and he felt there was no way to get the pieces together again. "Like Humpty Dumpty," he laughed mirthlessly. The voice on the other end of the crisis hotline invited him to come to church the next morning. As he entered the church door, he wasn't sure just what to expect. How could strangers help?

Yet during the next hour, those strangers did help. They greeted him warmly, actually listened when he shared, and took him out to lunch after church. During the afternoon, he joined several members for tennis at a local high school and returned for evening service and the afterglow at a member's house. That night as he fell asleep, Alan marveled at the feelings of warmth and peace that lingered as the result of the day.

The key to a successful ministry with people is providing warmth and acceptance for those who attend. The most effective outreach program is virtually useless if those you reach come to your group and find a lack of love. Few of your visitors will feel a desire to return unless they find that your group fills a need in their lives. And the most basic need you can fill is the need for loving acceptance during difficult times.

Therefore, one of your basic objectives is to plan to provide an atmosphere of love and acceptance that can be felt by first-time visitors as well as by each member. When your group is small, this atmosphere is easier to create and monitor. Each member assumes the responsibility for making people realize that they are cared for by sharing together, listening, going out for pie and coffee after church, and inviting visitors to share lunch. Visitors are easily noticed in small groups where all of the regular members know each other. Also in small groups, members know one another well enough to recognize the signs of personal struggles and can take time to go aside and share on a personal basis. Sharing in the down times as well as in the victorious moments is an important characteristic of a caring friend. Small groups have the advantage over large groups in fostering deep friendships among members.

Here are some ways you can pay attention to individuals even if your group is large.

Have a registration table

Ask your members to take turns handling visitor registration at a table near the door of your meeting room. The registration card can obtain a variety of information about your visitors such as name, address, age group, status (never married, divorced, or widowed), hobbies, interests, or occupation. Provide a name tag for visitors. Mark the visitor name tags so people are easily identified as first-timers.

Mail postcards to visitors

You may choose to send postcards or personal notes to first-time visitors to let them know you're glad they came. However, don't buy a hundred identical cards stamped "Glad you came!" The key to sending a card is making it a personal contact. This same principle holds true for birthday cards. A personal contact can bring a moment of happiness into someone's life while an impersonal contact rarely will!

Introduce visitors during meetings

Take a few minutes to introduce your visitors in each meeting. Have each one stand while you read the name, hobbies, interests, and occupation to the group. Members will then know something about each visitor and will have a basis for conversation after the meeting.

Plan a Sunday brunch

You can facilitate getting acquainted with visitors by having brunch together after church on Sunday mornings. The brunch can be coordinated in a number of ways. Some groups have a potluck or picnic where members bring their own food plus a little extra for visitors who are invited to attend as guests. In other groups, the members take turns cooking brunch for the group (either in the church kitchen or at home). Visitors are invited as guests and members pay only $2 a person. Still another method is to simply go to a local restaurant together after church, and each person orders and pays for his or her own meal. The disadvantages are that the meals are often expensive and arrangements have to be made ahead of time with the restaurant if large groups attend the brunches.

BE REAL

It is important that efforts to communicate warmth, love, and acceptance be genuine. God's love for us is genuine and so must ours be for others. It cost God a lot to demonstrate love for us, and it is our responsibility to pass it on. Jesus clearly gave us a commandment to love one another (John 13:34–35).

CHECK YOUR OUTREACH

✔ 1. Do you have written materials that publicize your ministry?

✔ 2. Is the quality of your publicity good or poor?

✔ 3. What methods are you using to share information about your ministry with the unreached single adults in your community?

✔ 4. Is there a sense of warmth and acceptance in your ministry?

✔ 5. Do you have an active plan for following up with visitors?

If these questions have helped you identify areas in which you could improve your ministry, take action today!

Part III

Provide Good Leadership

chapter 10

RECRUIT KEY LEADERS

Dan straightened up after placing the last chair in just the right place and surveyed the meeting room. Everything looked fine. The light on the coffee pot had just come on indicating that the brew was ready. The cups, sugar, creamer, stirrers, and napkins were in place. A plate of inviting doughnuts sat ready for sampling. The calendar of activities for the next month (which he had picked up from the printer on his way from work) was available on a table by the door, along with name tags and felt-tipped pens. Dan took a deep breath and let it out slowly as he looked at his watch. He had about five minutes to quickly review his notes for the lesson he would be teaching tonight. Or so he thought. At that minute, the first two single adults arrived, and Dan hurried over to greet them.

Later that night, after teaching the class, listening to several people tell about their experiences during the week, spending a half hour counseling one of the single men, straightening up the meeting room, washing out the coffee pot, and locking up, Dan drove home. He was exhausted.

Sometimes, after a particularly trying day at work, the tasks of being a lay leader for a single adult group in his church seemed overwhelming. Dan wondered why he continued in the role. It was really too much to ask of one person.

Then Dan would remember the joy he experienced when someone shared about a success during the week, when someone made a breakthrough emotionally and began the road to recovery from the grief of having lost a spouse, or when someone acknowledged to him that if it were not for the group, suicide would have been a genuine option. Then Dan knew why he was active in the ministry. The immediate rewards were sometimes exciting, and the eternal rewards were incomparable.

In the beginning of a ministry with single adults, most of the work, even the small tasks, are left to one or two leaders. It can get tiring.

The Ministry Team

Every ministry needs a designated leader, paid or volunteer. This leader is accountable to the congregational leadership for how that ministry functions. However, the actual organizational structure and the approach to leadership taken will vary by individual leader.

Some people shy away from organization of any form. Perhaps in the past they have experienced a destructive overemphasis on organization. But operating without any organization results in confusion, chaos, and ineffectiveness.

Every single adult ministry requires just enough organization to prevent confusion and no more. The amount of organization you'll want will depend on the size and scope of your own individual group. The purpose of organizing your group is to limit the responsibility assigned to any one person or committee. The purpose of organization is to maximize effectiveness. As your program changes, your organization will adapt accordingly.

Most leaders recognize the value of having a "ministry team," a group of leaders who work together to effect the ministry. In most cases, this team is comprised of volunteers who have agreed to take on various aspects of the ministry. This ministry team also serves as an accountability group for the designated minister/leader and as a planning and designing committee. The group provides support for one another by listening, giving feedback, praying for one another, and building a commitment to one another and to the ministry as they work together.

Moses learned how important it was to have a team to help him. While Joshua was fighting Amalek, Moses was on the top of the hill holding his hands up. As long as Moses' hands were up, Israel was winning, but when his hands were down, Amalek won. Israel was only able to win the ultimate victory because Aaron and Hur came and stood beside Moses and held his hands up. Moses could not do it alone (Ex. 17:8–16).

No matter how large the ministry becomes, no matter how many paid staff persons you hire, the backbone of your leadership team will be the lay leaders. These are the people who coordinate activities, serve as greeters, follow-up with visitors and members, work with you in planning, staff various committees, and do any number of the many tasks involved in your ministry. Without these volunteers, the size and effectiveness of your ministry will be limited to what can be accomplished by one designated leader.

The Minister/Leader

Those churches that genuinely understand the needs of single adults and the importance of this ministry often designate a paid, staff position as a minister with single adults. Having someone on staff in this capacity gives a clear message that the congregation believes the needs of single adults are important. When there is someone at this level on staff, it is likely the ministry is supported financially and single adults enjoy equal status in the church.

However, not all churches choose to hire a minister with single adults, and some cannot afford to pay the salary for an additional minister. The leader in most churches is a volunteer lay leader. The title for that lay leader is different from group to group: minister, director, leader, coordinator, president, chairperson, or some other title may be preferred.

The minister/leader may have a variety of assigned tasks, but at the very least, this person:

- Guides the ministry team in planning, conducting, and evaluating the ministry

- Coordinates the development and ongoing evaluation and/or revision of the mission statement for ministry

- Recruits needed leaders, workers, resource people, and helpers for the single adult ministry

- Defines resources, equipment, and supplies needed by the ministry and works to obtain these

- Assists the ministry team in setting goals for the ministry

- Provides training needed by the ministry team in their particular tasks

- Coordinates the beginning of new programs within the single adult ministry

- Networks with the leaders of other ministries with single adults

- Schedules and conducts regular meetings and planning sessions with the ministry team

- Keeps the lines of communication open among the ministry team

- Serves as a liaison between the ministry team and church leaders, ensuring that there is good communication between these groups

- Has the overall responsibility for the program, finances, and activities of the ministry

- Ministers to the members of the ministry team on a personal and spiritual level

THE TEAM

As a group grows in numbers and as the activities and programs increase, it becomes necessary to assign responsibilities to additional people, and more "leaders" are added. Over the years, a structure is built and a rhythm develops for the activities of the ministry.

To determine the leaders you need, analyze your ministry. Each focus area will need a coordinator (and when possible, a co-coordinator), although at first several focus areas may be assigned to one person. Focus areas include, but are not limited to, Bible study, discipleship, discussion groups, publicity, socials, outreach, music and worship, practical needs assistance, finances, recovery groups, single parents, and children of single parents.

The exact tasks assigned to a designated leader will depend on how you decide to organize your ministry. However, here are some suggestions:

Bible study

Under the direction of the minister with single adults, the ministry leader, or the Sunday school superintendent, the Bible study coordinator:

- Either leads or appoints leaders for the single adult Sunday school class and any other Bible studies that meet throughout the week

- Chooses group Bible studies designed to encourage personal and spiritual growth

- Makes sure the Bible studies are creative and involve a variety of learning methods

- Either offers personal counseling and help to individual members or directs them to professional help, not only during the class session but also during the week

- Cooperates with the other members of the ministry team

- Develops skills as an instructor and/or helps the other Bible study leaders in skills-development

- Attends and participates in as many of the class functions as possible

- Attends the regular ministry team meetings and planning sessions

Discipleship coordinator

Under the direction of the minister/leader, the discipleship coordinator:

- Serves as liaison for the single adults with the discipleship coordinator for the entire church

- Ensures that materials and disciplers are available to and for the single adults

- Coordinates the development of specialized ministries such as ministries to men (by men) and ministries to women (by women) as well as one-to-one discipleship connections

- Identifies seminars and programs sponsored by other churches and groups that may be helpful to the spiritual development of the single adult members and makes the information available to the group

- Coordinates the gathering of Christian reading materials, audiocassettes, and videocassettes into a lending library for the single adults

- Coordinates the prayer chain for the group. May schedule special or regular prayer meeting times and lead these

- Attends the regular ministry team meetings and planning sessions

Discussion-group coordinator

Under the direction of the minister/leader, the discussion-group coordinator:

- Develops a list of topics to be addressed over a period of several weeks

- Recruits and trains discussion-group facilitators

- Develops (alone or with the facilitators) the discussion starter questions and statements to be used

- Ensures that the discussion starters are duplicated and provided for each meeting of the discussion groups

- Evaluates the success of the small-group discussion program

- Is responsible for the logistics, room set up, and coordination of the small-group discussions

- Attends the regular ministry team meetings and planning sessions

Publicity coordinator

Under the direction of the minister/leader, the publicity coordinator:

- Ensures that there is a printed calendar of activities for the group

- Obtains copies of calendars from other single adult ministry groups and makes appropriate information available to group members so that major functions can be enjoyed and shared

- Sends public service announcements about special events to local radio and television stations and newspapers

- Arranges for paid advertisements for unique events

- Sends copies of flyers about special events to the leaders of other single adult ministries in the area

- Is responsible for getting information about the single adult ministry into the church bulletin, mid-week mailer, newsletter, and calendar as appropriate

- Makes announcements during the classes and meetings about upcoming events

- Maintains and periodically updates the mailing list for members

- Coordinates the printing of a directory of members

- Provides information about the ministry to persons who call the church inquiring about what is available

- Attends the regular ministry team meetings and planning sessions.

Socials coordinator

Under the direction of the minister/leader, the socials coordinator:

- Schedules social activities including parties, dinners, potlucks, sports events, and holiday celebrations

- Recruits individual coordinators for each event to identify location, price, resources needed, and to get tickets purchased and sold, or other appropriate activities

- Ensures that all needed information is complete for each event and is given to the publicity coordinator for inclusion on the monthly calendar

- Circulates sign-up sheets for events and for volunteers to help with the events. Contacts these people to ensure that they are on target with their assignments

- Coordinates refreshments at social activities and the Sunday morning sessions and small-group discussions
- Attends the regular ministry team meetings and planning sessions

Outreach coordinator

Under the direction of the minister/leader, the outreach coordinator:

- Identifies and coordinates group activities to reach out to other single adults who do not attend the group
- Identifies and coordinates group efforts to become involved in helping people in the community such as the homeless, orphans, single parents, unemployed, and older adults who need help
- Obtains information about mission projects or single-adult missionaries the group could support
- Obtains information about short-term mission trips and presents this information to the group
- Coordinates mission projects or trips for the group
- Attends the regular ministry team meetings and planning sessions

Music and worship coordinator

Under the direction of the minister/leader, the music and worship coordinator:

- Plans the music and worship portion of the various meetings and services
- Recruits a music and worship team
- Arranges for appropriate methods of providing members with the words to songs
- Ensures that there is appropriate instrumental accompaniment for songs
- Attends the regular ministry team meetings and planning sessions

Practical-needs coordinator

Under the direction of the minister/leader, the practical-needs coordinator:

- Identifies the types of practical needs the group might consider focusing on such as child care, moving assistance, major yard work, providing hand-me-down clothing, a canned food closet, furniture exchange, rooms for rent, jobs listing, etc.
- Devises a way of making needs, as well as available resources, known to the group
- Coordinates work-project days during which members help one another
- Attends the regular ministry team meetings and planning sessions

Treasurer

Under the direction of the minister/leader, the treasurer:

- Maintains an accurate record of all monies collected and the disposition of these
- Maintains the checkbook for the ministry
- Pays the bills incurred by the group from group funds
- Provides periodic financial reports to the ministry team
- Attends the regular ministry team meetings and planning sessions

Secretary

Under the direction of the minister/leader, the secretary:

- Keeps minutes of all regular ministry team meetings and planning sessions
- Maintains the files and records for the ministry
- Makes copies of minutes, files, and reports as appropriate for the ministry team
- Receives telephone calls and directs callers to the appropriate ministry team member for information
- Attends the regular ministry team meetings and planning sessions

Special ministry coordinator

Under the direction of the minister/leader, the special ministry coordinator:

- Identifies and addresses the special ministries that are needed within the group (i.e., single parents, grief recovery, divorce recovery, addiction recovery, adult children of … groups)
- Identifies and recruits leaders for special ministries
- Assists special ministry leaders in obtaining the needed literature and resources for conducting the ministries
- Coordinates the special ministries
- Attends the regular ministry team meetings and planning sessions.

The Class or Subgroup President

The Sunday school class usually has a "president" with specifically assigned responsibilities. Often the functions of the "president" are fulfilled by the minister/leader until the group becomes large enough to divide into more classes or subgroups. Then an administrative leader (president) is needed for each class or subgroup. It is also common for each class or subgroup to have leaders in each of the focus areas listed above. These leaders would serve as committee members to the ministry team member assigned to that area. For example, the social coordinators for each class would serve as a social committee under the direction of the ministry team member designated as the social coordinator for the entire single adult ministry.

Under the direction of the minister/leader, the class or subgroup president:

- Plans the order of service for the Sunday morning meetings and may serve as a "master of ceremonies" each week

- Coordinates the activities of the class or subgroup along with the team of leaders for that class or subgroup
- Attends the regular ministry team meetings and planning sessions
- Conducts planning meetings with all the class leaders

Miscellaneous Duties

In addition to the above duties, there are always any number of miscellaneous duties that must be performed each week. Each of these should be assigned to one of the leaders or volunteers. Leaving these functions unassigned results either in confusion and chaos or causes one person to assume the responsibility for them all. These miscellaneous functions include such things as arranging the meeting room, making coffee, bringing refreshments, making announcements, closing windows and locking doors after class functions, cleaning up after socials, and running errands during the week.

LEADERSHIP QUALIFICATIONS

"What about Pete as president?" Sally asked. The nominating committee had met at her house that evening to begin discussing potential leaders for the upcoming term of office.

"Oh, no!" Tom asserted. "Pete is really struggling right now with some pretty heavy personal problems. Maybe in another six months he'll be ready to serve on the ministry team."

Not everyone in your single adult group is in a position to be a leader. Some are in more of a *learning* rather than a *leading* phase of their personal and spiritual development. There are usually higher standards for leaders than for group members because leaders are expected to be the models. In writing to Timothy, Paul explained this principle (1 Tim. 3:1–13). However, we do not have to wait until a person is totally grown up spiritually and emotionally before giving him or her a position of leadership, particularly one that doesn't involve teahing. Each member of the body of Christ is given spiritual gifts for the edification of the body, and we need to allow our single adults to use their gifts.

It is important that leaders are caring, approachable, committed to ministry, honest, courteous, and dependable.

RECRUITING LEADERS

Many ministries with single adults started because single adults felt a need for a unique, specialized ministry within the broader life of the church. The ministry grew because of the energy of those who wanted the ministry. The primary leadership role was probably assigned or assumed with a minimum of fuss.

However, finding the right leadership is always a challenge. Continue to watch people and plan whom you might recruit for a leadership role when an opening exists. A six-month term of office is usually a good time limit before giving a leader a chance to either reenlist, change assignments, or go off the leadership team for a few months. This helps resolve the problem of burnout, which is common in leaders within single adult ministries.

Married or single adults?

The minister/leader of a ministry with single adults can be either a married person, a married couple, or a single adult. The important thing to remember is that the leaders you want are those whom God has called to be leaders and who are willing to fulfill that calling. About half of the leaders/ministers in single adult ministries are married, not because this is a requirement of the church but because more and more people are catching the vision of the exciting possibilities for ministry with single adults. Often, but not always, the married leader is actually an "alumnus" having spent some time as a single or single-again adult. And all married adults were single at one time!

On the other hand, it is essential that some, even most, of the ministry team leaders are single or single-again adults. Ministering to others is an important step in the healing process for those recovering from the loss of a spouse. Not all single adults going through a loss situation or rejection experience will be ready or willing to relate to a married leader with the same receptivity as they might to a fellow single. Because ministry needs to be designed as one "with" single adults, singles need to be in positions of leadership.

Male or female?

There are more female leaders in single adult ministries than there are male leaders, partly because there are more single women than men. Use those leaders who can be effective in your group. But it is important that you attempt to have as many single men as possible in positions of leadership for several reasons. Serving in a leadership position is a developmental exercise and can increase a man's ability to be a spiritual leader. When single men visit the class or subgroup, they need to see other men up front and in leadership positions so they will feel comfortable and come back. You will want to have good, strong, single men who are good leaders, who can help you design and effect a ministry with single men where their needs can be met in a safe way.

When approaching potential leaders, you need to have a plan.

1. Ask God to guide you in recruiting leaders so you will notice and approach those who are gifted and ready to make the necessary commitment to lead.

2. Have clearly defined and written job descriptions for each position of leadership in your group. These duty statements provide a basis for discussing the possibilities for service and expectations.

3. Be very clear about your expectations. How many hours a week do you need the person to commit to the ministry? How many meetings a month? What exactly is the person agreeing to do?

4. Look for single adults who have demonstrated a gift for leadership and administration in any area of their lives, at home, on the job, in previous church experience, or in the community.

5. Approach people with a positive attitude. You are offering people an opportunity to use their God-given talents and to grow. Don't try to make people feel it is their duty to be a leader. Don't make the person feel guilty if the answer is "no." Remember that God is guiding you to the right people, and when you find them, you also will discover that their hearts will have been prepared by the Holy Spirit to listen to your offer and to respond with a "yes."

6. When appropriate, recruit a man and a woman for co-coordinators. This helpful approach means one person doesn't have to do everything.

SELECTING LEADERS

Every church or organization will have its own procedures for selecting and appointing leaders. The most common include recruiting candidates (which sometimes includes using a nominating committee), verifying that applicants meet an established qualification standard, interviewing all candidates, and final selection by member voting or executive appointment.

Interviewing potential leaders is one method of assessing candidate qualifications and the appropriateness of appointments. Interviews may be conducted by a nominating committee, the minister/leader, the director of Christian education, or the pastor. Whoever conducts the interviews needs to plan questions that will give the interviewees the opportunity to present themselves and their qualifications. Questions you might ask include:

- Why are you interested in a leadership position at this time?

- What experiences have you had that enable you to be an effective ministry team member in our ministry?

- Describe your leadership style and approach.

- What are your leadership gifts and strengths?

- What experiences have you had as a member of a leadership team?

- Describe your personal relationship with God.

- Share a recent experience that helped you grow spiritually.

- How much time could you devote each week to the position?

- How would you hope to grow as a person through this leadership experience?

- What would you like to tell us about yourself?

Develop additional or substitute questions to fit your needs. Conduct the interviews in an appropriate location. If there are several applicants, you might use a business-like approach, asking candidates to come to an office, one at a time, and be interviewed. If you are seeking the assistance of a particular person for a specific leadership role, you might "interview" in a home, over a cup of coffee in a quiet restaurant, or in the office.

After you have interviewed potential leaders, pray that God will guide you in making your final choice.

IT'S A NEVER-ENDING FUNCTION

Recruiting new leaders is a never-ending function. Leaders burn out, get transferred, start dating someone who attends another church, move away, get married and decide that they no longer want to be involved in single adult ministry, and sometimes just quit. Keep your eyes open and always be on the alert for potential leaders for your ministry.

CHECK YOUR RECRUITING

✔ 1. Do you have defined leadership positions?

✔ 2. Do you have written job descriptions?

✔ 3. Do you have a recruiting strategy?

✔ 4. Do you have a selection process?

✔ 5. Do you already have a list of leaders who are ready to step into vacancies that might occur?

✔ 6. Are you always on the lookout for potential leaders?

If these questions have helped you identify areas in your ministry that need improvement, take action today!

chapter 11

Empower Your Leaders

"I've been active in the church for most of my life, ever since high school," Devin commented. *"This is the first time I've actually enjoyed the experience. Our single adult minister makes sure we have what we need to get the job done and gives us the freedom to do a job without always making sure we do it his way."*

Devin is an empowered leader.

Recruiting leaders is only the first step in building a leadership team. The next step involves empowering the team. Empowering includes clarifying needs, fleshing out the vision, equipping, and stepping back.

The Temptation of Leadership

The biggest temptation in leadership is to maintain tight control over every aspect of the ministry. Control is important to most people in leadership positions because these people generally like order and have a clear idea of how they want things done. Therefore, it is natural that a minister/leader would want to control the ministry.

Controlling people want to control because they do not want to fail. They control because they want things done their way. They may control because they don't want to let people see their weaknesses, and with control, they can cover them up. And they control because they are afraid of rejection if something doesn't go right.

There are ways of exercising strict control in ministry. Leaders may retain the decision-making authority and refuse to delegate. They don't share information, which ensures that they are the persons to whom others come when they need to know something. They develop several contingency plans to implement in case something goes awry. They control group discussions by letting people know their ideas first, which discourages additional sharing. They sometimes control by procrastinating so that they are the only ones who can save the day by a last-minute deed or decision. And they control others by withholding affirmation or encouragement when someone begins to exercise individual creativity or initiative.

The first step in sharing control and understanding the value of *team* leadership is understanding your goal for ministry. Dr. John Westfall says your answer to a couple of key questions will determine your approach to ministry.

Is it your goal to build strong ministries?_____

Or

Is it your goal to build strong people who minister?_____

Depending on which of these two goals you are committed to, you will automatically allocate your time, energy, and activities in one of two directions: toward completing the task or toward developing people.

If you are focused on completing the task, some people will probably develop new skills in the process but at a minimal level. If you focus on developing people, the task will probably get done to some degree but not necessarily the way you had in mind. You get to choose which outcome is more important for you in your ministry.

If your goal as the minister/leader is to build strong people who minister with single adults, you will need to focus on the tasks of leadership.

TASK #1: CLARIFYING NEEDS

When someone comes to you and says that a new area of ministry is needed, your job is to help clarify the need. Is the idea just an idea or a way of meeting a genuine need? Help people clarify their ideas and identify the scope of needs by asking investigative questions. Examples include:

• Why do you think we should do this?

• What exactly is the need as you see it?

• When does this need exist?

• Who is experiencing the need?

• Where do we begin to meet the need?

• How can we meet this need?

If people can't give you good answers to these questions, ask that they do research or additional thinking. Meet with them again at a later date to discuss the issue and see if the need has been clearly identified and the ideas for meeting the need carefully thought-out. Thinking through ideas and wrestling with issues help people develop a commitment to the project and take ownership of the plan. It keeps you, as the minister/leader, from doing all the work.

Task #2: Fleshing Out the Vision

Once the need has been clearly defined and an idea developed that will meet the need, your next role is to assist your leaders in fleshing out the vision of the new area of ministry. Again, asking questions is the key to encouraging them to see the possibilities. Here are some helpful questions you can ask:

- Is this need just a local issue, or is it also present on a broader level?

- If money were no object, what would be your dream for meeting the need?

- If you were an expert, what would you do to resolve this need?

- What have you done in the past that would be similar to what you will do to meet this need?

- What will the results of the project be?

- What will happen if you don't meet this need here and now?

- What obstacles do you anticipate?

- What will you do to overcome those specific obstacles?

- What setbacks can you anticipate?

- What can you do to minimize the setbacks?

- What do you need to get started?

As people answer these and other similar questions, they begin to actually plan the details of the new ministry and get involved in the project. The more questions you ask up front and the more answers they develop, the further along the planning process will be.

Task #3: Equipping the Team

In your role as minister/leader, you will sometimes be a coach, sometimes a player, and sometimes an equipment manager. Once you have leaders ready to move out and get involved in beginning new ministries, you function to ensure they are equipped for the task. First comes training, if necessary.

Training and developing your leaders is an ongoing process. New leaders will want to learn the details of your organizational structure and processes and the purpose and strategies of each function and activity. All leaders require constant upgrading of their personal and group interaction skills and leadership abilities so that the program will grow. Special-function committee chairpersons will require special training to develop competence in their assigned jobs.

Providing training for leaders takes many forms. First, determine what type of training is needed. Ask the leaders to determine what deficiencies they feel or experience. Then plan and provide the appropriate training to meet the needs. If one of the leaders lacks some specific knowledge, provide reading materials, demonstrations, information sessions, workshops, or seminars.

If a leader lacks a skill, provide information in one of the above ways and then provide opportunities to practice the skill under supervision and then alone.

Training resources are readily available in most communities. Bookstores and libraries provide books, magazines, and films. Colleges provide leadership courses. Seminars are sponsored by various organizations on topics relevant to a leader in a single adult ministry. Experienced leaders are usually willing to share with neophytes in a one-to-one situation. Become creative and plan and conduct your own leadership-training conference.

After training comes coaching. You can contribute your own ideas to brainstorming sessions, give appropriate information, and assist with negotiating the bureaucracy within your church. Some policies and procedures are non-negotiable and must be followed. Others can be changed through the proper channels. Projects may require some restrictions, and these need to be stated up front to avoid frustration at a later date. In your role as coach, provide insight. Because it is easier for an uninvolved person to step back and see the bigger picture, that becomes your responsibility. Be willing to say, "Here's how I envision the outcome of your present course."

After coaching comes providing resources. It is your responsibility to assist in finding funding, equipment, space, literature, organizations, and transportation that will facilitate the implementation of the vision and the project. This is not to say you must do all the work of procuring, but you must know how to go about doing so and point others in the right direction to obtain what is needed.

After providing resources, you become a cheerleader. Provide affirmation, encouragement, and lots of praise. Be quick to give the credit for a success, a project, a dream, and a good result to your leaders.

TASK #4: EMPOWERING THE TEAM

When one of your goals is to develop strong people, you will find it necessary to sometimes step back out of their way when they get moving on a project, a new ministry, or assuming a new leadership role. The power of the Holy Spirit working within your individual leaders will produce incredible results within the ministry. The Spirit will make your ministry team successful.

When you step out of the way, and are willing to release your leaders to minister in the power of the Holy Spirit, you are in effect aiding in the empowering of people. There are three ways you can affirm your leaders.

Give them the freedom to act

Give people decision-making authority whenever possible within the limits you have to set because of church policy and procedures.

Stand behind your leaders

When things don't go right, be the first to step in and take the responsibility even while supporting your team and the ideas they were attempting to implement.

Believe in your leaders

Show your leaders you believe in them. They can do whatever you believe they can do. Empower your team by believing in them.

Task #5: Building the Team

Once you have a group of leaders, you need to ensure that you build a team. There is a world of difference between a group of people and a team! A team is *an interdependent group of people working closely together toward a common goal, agreeing upon assigned member responsibilities and standards.* Teamwork doesn't just happen; it is the result of careful planning and hard work. Let's take apart the definition and see what steps to take.

Interdependent group of people

Interdependency can be developed when people realize that each is responsible for only a part of the whole task of leading the single adult ministry. It is important that no one position be seen as super significant while others are considered inferior. Another way to encourage interdependency is to include all leaders in the planning meetings, in policy making, decision making, and problem solving. Try consensus in decision making rather than majority rule. Discourage destructive power plays among members of the ministry team.

Working closely together

Monthly planning meetings, shared responsibilities, and frequent communication keep your leaders working closely together.

Toward a common goal

At the beginning of each term of office, have each group of leaders review and discuss the objectives of the single adult ministry so they can all agree on goals. Adopt new objectives as a group.

Agreeing upon assigned member responsibilities

Providing each leader with an individual job description simplifies the division of responsibilities. Leaders can agree upon the assignment of little extra duties.

Standards

Setting team ground rules is an important group task. Everyone needs to know what policies, procedures, and rules to follow. Some teams agree members may say anything they wish (in confidence) at planning meetings. Other teams agree that no member will complain without offering a suggestion for correcting the problem. Whatever ground rules are adopted, it is important that each team member abide by them.

Developing team spirit among your leaders is essential because the quality of the teamwork directly influences the success of your single adult ministry.

TASK #6: IDENTIFYING PROBLEMS IN THE TEAM

Problems caused by jealousies, conflicts, or competition often surface within a team. The signs may include: missing team meetings, criticizing one another, snipping at one another, open fighting, withholding of information or support, sabotage of each other's work, gossip about one another, or asking to be relieved of a leadership role.

Your job as minister/leader is to work with the individuals involved to resolve issues. Simply reminding everyone of the mission of your single adult ministry may effect change. However, when problems erupt out in the open, solutions are usually more complicated. Try getting the individuals together. Encourage a respectful discussion of issues. Show team members how to make "contracts" to treat one another with dignity and respect. Facilitate forgiveness. In the process, remember to speak the truth in love, to be gentle even when being firm (Eph. 4:15).

CHECK YOUR EMPOWERING

✔ 1. Do you retain total control in your single adult ministry?

✔ 2. What is your goal for ministry? To build a strong ministry? Or to build strong people who minister?

✔ 3. How good are you at helping people clarify their dreams?

✔ 4. How good are you at helping people flesh out their dreams?

✔ 5. How do you equip your leaders?

✔ 6. How do you consciously empower your leaders?

✔ 7. What systems do you have in place for bonding your leaders together into a team?

✔ 8. What systems do you have in place to identify problems within your team?

✔ 9. How successful have you been in resolving team problems?

If these questions have helped you identify areas in which you could improve your ministry, take action today!

Part IV

Expand to Meet Needs

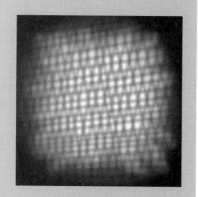

chapter 12

HOST SPECIAL EVENTS

Karen hummed a happy tune as she finished grading the last stack of exam papers and prepared to leave the office.

"You sure seem cheerful, even for a Friday afternoon," a fellow teacher commented. "Big plans for this weekend?"

"You bet! Our single adult group is going to the mountains," Karen replied.

"Seems as if you're always doing something special with those single adult friends of yours," her friend said.

"They're a special group, all right!"

Make your single adult program special by organizing extra events such as retreats, concerts, workshops, conferences, and holiday celebrations.

PLAN A RETREAT

Later that evening, several of the single adults from Karen's group wandered through the campsites offering assistance to any of the participants who were having trouble setting up tents, getting lanterns to light, or starting campfires. From one of the campsites, strains of guitar music and singing floated through the night. The scent of pine filled the air, and in the darkening sky, early stars shone. What a wonderful beginning to a Labor Day weekend camp-out.

Getting away from daily life as a group is something most single adult groups enjoy. And with planning, almost any single adult group (from eight to 1,000 members) can have a successful retreat.

Why have a retreat?

What triggers a weekend retreat? Here are a few of the many reasons for planning a retreat:

- *To organize and train leaders*—Getting together makes it possible to discuss roles, responsibilities, policies, procedures, plans, and objectives.

- *To build group spirit*—Getting away together gives people a chance to share together in a special way as they pray, play, and work together.

- *To be inspired*—Sometimes getting away from the routine of life gives people a chance to get in touch with God and to respond to the Spirit's leading in their lives.

- *To be strengthened in the inner self*—Relaxing and listening to God's voice gives peace and strength to the inner self and an opportunity to get in touch with one's feelings and needs.

- *To have fun*—Having fun with other Christians can be a valid reason to plan a retreat to the mountains, beach, country, lake, or woods.

Where do you start?

To be successful and achieve your objectives, you will want to carefully plan your retreat. Here are steps to take:

❏ Determine your objective for the retreat.

The purpose for having the retreat will determine the other steps you take, the schedule you set, the people you invite, and the publicity you give the event.

❏ Discover what your single adults want or need.

Get input from your single adults before planning a retreat. If no one enjoys camping, your retreat location will need to be where there are sufficient modern conveniences.

❏ Plan well in advance.

Select a date and a time with enough advance notice for your adults to plan ahead. Allow enough time for them to save up for the cost of the retreat. If you are reserving public campsites or space at a retreat center, you may have to give up to a year's notice to get reservations for the more popular holiday weekends such as Labor Day, Memorial Day, and the Fourth of July.

❏ Select an appropriate location.

Some of the places you may consider holding retreats include: local campgrounds, city parks and recreation sites, Boy Scout camps, church camps, Christian conference grounds, church-owned colleges (during summer months), or a friendly farmer's meadow!

❏ Plan the agenda and schedule.

Although your purpose for the retreat will determine your schedule and agenda, there are some basics to remember such as wake up, personal devotions, meals, free time, group activities, meetings, sessions, and workshops. Be sure to vary the activities. Don't plan for people to spend 12 hours a day sitting in seminars. And don't just have a camp-out where people are on their own for the entire weekend. Find the right balance.

Some retreats may be highly structured, and others may allow a lot of free time. A retreat to the mountains might include such activities as a pancake breakfast, hiking, sunrise devotions, swimming, campfire talks, hymn sing-alongs, arts and crafts, hot dog roasts, and sharing and prayer times. A leadership training retreat might include a challenging kickoff message on commitment, workshops on leadership roles, discussions of handout materials, question-and-answer times with present and past leaders, planning meetings, and a few games such as Frisbee, softball, and pillow fighting.

When planning several retreats during the year, vary the types you hold. Some might include children, but when this is done, be sure to have super-vised activities for the children during the times the adults are expected to be involved in seminars or workshops. The activities for the children may include sports, nature walks, games, arts and crafts, and videos.

❑ Select a good speaker.

Get a good speaker for any retreat you plan. You will probably want to have a keynote speaker and two or more workshops depending on the purpose of the weekend. If possible, try to secure a speaker whose repu-tation will draw your single adults and who is an effective communicator. This might be your own pastor, professors at a local church or commu-nity college, pastors from other churches, a minister with single adults, a celebrity, a Christian counsellor, or an author. Although you may be able to obtain a speaker who will waive the honorarium, you usually need to plan on paying a speaker. Because speakers' fees vary considerably, be sure to check this out carefully *before* you make arrangements.

❑ Keep the cost affordable.

Because you want as many people as possible to attend your retreat, and because single adults do not have a fortune to spend on retreats, you will need to keep the cost as low as possible and still provide a quality week-end. Discuss what is an acceptable standard of quality for your single adults. Some people are perfectly comfortable with a camping weekend where everyone brings food and helps with the preparation of the meals. Some groups not only want indoor beds and plumbing but well-cooked meals served in a nice dining room.

Total the cost of the retreat (location charges, meals, speakers' fees, pub-licity, materials, and other miscellaneous items) and add a cushion of 10 percent. Divide the total by the number of single adults you anticipate will attend (don't over-estimate), and you have the individual cost of the retreat. The 10 percent cushion will allow you to cover unexpected costs.

Some groups give partial or full scholarships to single adults who simply cannot afford the cost of the retreat. Usually it is best if a single adult pays part of the cost, if at all possible, so there is a personal investment.

Scholarships are paid out of the church or single adult treasury, from special offerings, or from special donations to the scholarship fund. Encourage scholarship recipients to "repay" the fund at a later date, if possible, so that other single adults may benefit as needed.

❑ Publicize your retreat.

Put together a brochure or flyer about the retreat listing the schedule, location, directions for getting there, items participants need to bring, cost, and telephone numbers for the retreat coordinator in case of questions.

Make announcements at each of your single adult functions well in advance of the retreat so people will have time to plan to attend. ***NOTE:*** *It is wise to give an early registration discount on the cost. It will encourage making a commitment early enough for you to let the retreat center know about how many people you will have.* About five or six months in advance, announce the idea. Three months in advance begin taking reservations and deposits. Four to six weeks in advance begin taking reservations in earnest.

❑ Enjoy yourself.

Once you are at the retreat, some things will always go wrong. Don't get caught in the "if only" game. Relax and enjoy what goes well. Learn from your mistakes, and in time, you can become a genuine expert in planning successful retreats.

SPONSOR A CONFERENCE

Seven hundred voices filled the sanctuary with the beautiful melody of "We Are One in the Spirit" at the annual single adult conference of a large church. Participants had come from all over the state to share together as they learned secrets for living the single life, developing creative talents, and starting new ministries with single adults.

At the end of the two-day conference, participants had made new friends, shared an inestimable amount of information, and went away tired but challenged.

Why have a conference?

Conferences can be planned for most of the same reasons you have retreats and workshops—to educate, train, motivate, unify, inspire, and encourage. However, the conference format has a few unique characteristics and advantages over retreats and workshops:

- *Explores a theme*—A conference on a particular theme, topic, or group of related subjects brings together different "experts" to address the topic(s) from various approaches.

- *Meets several different levels of needs*—A conference where different "tracks" are held allows participants to decide which track to attend (i.e., starting single adult ministries, expanding single adult ministries, and special single adult ministries).

- *Draws and ministers to a large lumber of people*—A conference with a keynote speaker and workshops that are repeated several times gives people a choice of workshops to attend. This format also allows the size of the workshops to be more manageable.

- *Shares resources*—A conference can be sponsored by several different ministries and leaders.

A conference is primarily educational so there is little free time planned, no sports or recreational activities, and meals are planned to conserve time and be as efficient as possible.

Where do you start?

Planning a conference can get complicated so be sure to start early.

❏ Identify the purpose for the conference.

Determine the audience for whom the conference will be planned, (leaders, single adults, single parents, single men). Decide on the theme of the conference and give it a title that communicates the theme.

❏ Determine the format and schedule for the conference.

Determine the length of the conference and the time schedule for each day. Be sure to allow enough time for coffee and stretch breaks and for personal interaction between the participants. A typical agenda might look like this:

8:00	Registration
8:30	**General Session #1**
9:45	Break
10:00	Select one of several special workshops
11:30	Lunch
12:30	**General Session #2**
1:45	Break
2:00	Select one of several special workshops
3:30	Break
3:45	Select one of several special workshops
5:00	Dinner (or dinner break)
6:30	Sing-a-long
7:00	**General Session #3**
8:30	Small-group discussions
10:00	Adjourn to local coffee shop for fellowship or go home

❏ Set the dates for your conference.

Select a couple dates for the conference and verify the availability of the desired location (your church, a community room or center, or a school or college campus). Check with your church calendar to ensure that no major conflict exists.

❏ Select speakers.

Locate good speakers or presenters for the general sessions and the workshops. Usually one keynote speaker does all the general sessions. Contact the keynote speaker and see if the proposed dates are possible.

❏ Publicize your conference.

Design an attractive brochure or flyer to publicize the conference. Depending on the purpose for the conference, give it the widest possible publicity. If it is for single adults in general, send copies of the flyer or brochure to other churches and follow-up with personal telephone calls to the leaders of other single adult ministries. Do special mailings to people who have attended conferences in the past. Use whatever free advertising is available through your local radio and television stations and newspapers.

❏ Remember the basics.

Meals are important. To keep the cost of the conference as low as possible, you may allow time for participants to arrange for their own meals off site during meal breaks. If you choose this alternative, allow more time for the meals and provide a map of places to eat in the neighborhood. You also can serve lunch and/or supper at the conference. Volunteers can cook, serve, and clean up. Include the cost of the meal(s) in the registration charge. Snacks are not essential, but they are a nice touch. During breaks, you can provide light refreshment for participants.

Another consideration is lodging. If out-of-town participants are expected, you can ask your single adults to open their homes (free of charge) to conference guests. Or you can provide a map of local motels.

Transportation may be an issue if there are large numbers of out-of-town participants. Try to provide a shuttle service.

Directions are important. Clearly mark workshop rooms with the titles of the workshops and the times they are held. Provide a site map with registration materials indicating where each workshop will be held. Try to keep changes to a minimum. Also indicate where restroom facilities and pay phones are located.

❏ Keep costs affordable.

The conference costs must be reasonable for one-income single adults. Develop your budget, add a 10 percent cushion, and divide by a reasonable number of expected conference participants to determine the individual conference fee. Provide scholarships when needed and practical.

❏ Provide hosts and hostesses.

Arrange for several of your single adults to serve as hosts and hostesses to greet, escort, and assist participants and speakers during the conference. One of the greatest keys to a successful conference is to communicate a spirit of helpfulness and warmth for each guest. Challenge your single adults to experience the blessings of reaching out and serving others during a conference. Set up a speakers' lounge with snacks and hot and cold drinks.

❑ Provide registration materials.

Prepare a registration packet including a schedule, workshop information, site map, blank paper for note taking, information about optional activities during free time (if any), biographical information on speakers, a brochure about your single adult ministry, and any other information that is appropriate such as an audiocassette order form if you are recording the sessions.

❑ Set up a resource center.

Invite appropriate groups or persons to set up information tables. These might include a book table from your local bookstore, single adult ministries from different churches, audiocassette selling table, tables where speakers may sell their books if they are authors, and information on other resources related to the theme of the conference.

HAVE A CONCERT

You may decide to have a concert, or a series of concerts, sponsored by your single adult ministry. The concert is an excellent outreach activity that can introduce single adults from your community to your group and your church.

If you vary the type of music you provide, and provide quality programs, you may be surprised at just how successful you can be. One large church decided to do Saturday night concerts once a month and see what would happen. Their first few involved local artists and the attendance varied from 100 to 250 single adults. However, within a year they were booking headline Christian artists and the attendance averaged more than 2,000 per event! For that church, in that community, the idea was perfect.

Why have concerts?

There are several reasons to have concerts:

- *To entertain*—Christians can get together and have fun enjoying good music.

- *To reach unchurched single adults*—Often a person will come to a concert even if nothing else could induce church attendance.

- *To present the message of Jesus Christ*—Music is a different but effective way of presenting the message of the Gospel of Jesus Christ to the world.

- *To encourage and uplift*—Music can often encourage, inspire, and uplift the spirit of those who have had a difficult day or week.

Where do you begin?

You begin slowly!

❑ Identify local Christian artists.

Discover the Christian artists and musicians in your area and go hear them. Select a few who might be successful in drawing a good-sized audience. Contact them and determine their fees and availability.

❏ Select the site.

You will want a location conducive to a concert, with an adequate sound system and comfortable seating. Once you find the location, determine the availability and rental fee (if any). When the arrangements are made, set the date for your first concert.

❏ Decide on the cost.

Because you are committed to paying for the musicians and artists, you may want to sell tickets in advance and at the door. You also can collect a freewill offering. Whatever way you decide to raise the money for the event, you will need to be sure that you have enough in the treasury to pay for the concert if incoming funds are insufficient.

❏ Publicize your event.

Often the quality of an event is prejudged by the quality of the publicity pieces. Take this into consideration when planning publicity. Use all available publicity avenues to get the word out about your concert.

OFFER SEMINARS

Seminars are informational sessions on a particular topic. These are usually one-day or one-evening events, but you might schedule a short series of seminars that would run once a week for several weeks.

Why have seminars?

Seminars can assist you in meeting several different objectives:

* *To educate*—Participants explore any one of a variety of topics in-depth, covering different viewpoints. Therefore, the seminar can assist with personal or spiritual growth.

* *To train*—The seminar provides information and opportunities to acquire specific skills (assertiveness, communication, leadership) and techniques.

* *To motivate*—The seminar can stimulate people to make positive life changes or create excitement about sharing their faith with others.

Where do you begin?

When planning a seminar, follow many of the same steps for organizing a retreat or a conference.

❏ Determine the need.

Have your single adults expressed an interest in learning more about a certain topic? Have you observed a need for skills development with the group?

❏ Decide the length of the seminar.

A Saturday seminar might be for three hours in the morning or afternoon, or it could go all day. A weekend seminar might begin on Friday evening and continue through Saturday afternoon. An evening seminar might be for only two hours.

❏ Select a speaker, date, time, and location.

Arrange for a speaker and settle on a date, time, and location for the seminar. Determine the cost of the seminar. Seminars are easily held in classroom facilities at the church or at a school. The formality of these kinds of facilities can be offset by using a variety of participative-learning techniques and establishing a warm and friendly climate for the seminar.

❏ Arrange for child care.

Don't forget to arrange for child care during the seminar so that your single parents can attend.

❏ Keep the cost affordable.

As with the other special events, you will want to keep the cost affordable for your single adults.

BE CREATIVE

The key to successful special events is to allow your creativity to flow.

Use holidays as an excuse to get together and do something special such as having a formal banquet with tuxedos and gowns, feeding a large group of the homeless, or holding a unique celebration.

Consider adapting the popular talk show format for a regular Saturday evening event. This approach may increase attendance in an exciting way.

Hosting cultural evenings and staging plays and musicals are other ideas single adult ministries have used as a way of reaching out to other single adults while drawing their own members closer together.

CHECK YOUR EVENTS

✔ 1. What special events have you hosted?

✔ 2. How might you adapt special events you have attended?

✔ 3. What special events would your single adults attend?

✔ 4. What special events do your single adults need?

If these questions have helped you identify areas in which you could improve your ministry, take action today!

chapter 13

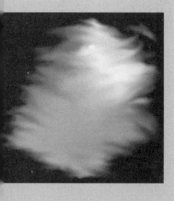

REACH SINGLE MEN

"How can we get more single men to come to our group?" Annette asked, voicing a question that others in the group lacked the courage to raise.

It's not an uncommon question. Most single adult groups are comprised mostly of women at about a two to one (or sometimes even higher) ratio to men. Realistically, you will probably always have more women than men for several reasons. First, there are simply more single women than single men in the United States. Second, women tend to remain single longer than men after a divorce or the death of a spouse. Third, women are more apt to look for affirmation, understanding, and healing from an available single adult ministry than are men.

But the real question is not how to get more men into the group, the real question is: *How can we minister to the needs of single men?*

Single men have identity struggles, self-esteem concerns, rejection hurts, and experience loneliness just like single women. However, while it is acceptable for women to open up emotionally and tell others about their inner struggles, fears, dreams, and hurts, it is not totally acceptable, or comfortable, for some men. Therefore, participating in groups or activities that encourage emotional openness and honesty may not be something for which your single men are ready.

If single men won't be open about their needs and hurts, how can you minister with them?

PLAN PHYSICAL ACTIVITIES

Before you can meet the needs of single men, you will need to get them to attend some of your functions so they can begin to feel comfortable with the members of your group. The best way to accomplish this is to provide physical activities. These are usually nonthreatening to someone who wants to remain emotionally withdrawn at first. Such activities might include: work days at church or on members' cars or homes; swimming, biking, hiking, or skiing trips; volleyball, softball, baseball, basketball, racquetball, or handball games; or attending football, baseball, basketball, or hockey games.

One of the best activities for single adult groups with sporadic attendance is a weekly volleyball night. Set up one or more courts, and begin the games when as few as four people show up. You can be a bit loose with the rules, and people will have fun hitting the ball back and forth until enough people arrive to have a real game. Volleyball is fairly simple and doesn't require tremendous skill, so anyone can have fun. If there is a set night for volleyball each week, a person doesn't have to make a commitment to attend or plan well in advance. When that night arrives, the person knows where they can find people playing volleyball and having fun.

When people are involved in physical activities there is little pressure to open up and share what is going on inside their heads and hearts. It is a safe way to be with people without the threat of having one's privacy invaded. Thus, single adults, especially men who may want to be with others and have fun, feel safe in coming to a physically demanding activity. They may become regular attendees of other group functions as well.

Over a period of several weeks, men who have attended the group to participate in physical group activities may develop friendships among the members. They may begin to feel comfortable enough to open up on an individual basis or even in a small-group discussion.

DEVELOP MALE LEADERSHIP

It is important for single men to see other men in leadership positions. This doesn't mean that there can't be women in leadership, even in key positions. Avoid giving the impression that this is a women's group because *all* of your speakers, leaders, officers, and announcement makers are women. If you don't have strong male leaders, consider recruiting a gifted male leader (this might be a single or a married man). Also develop the leadership potential of one or more of your inexperienced men.

MAKE THEM FEEL WELCOME

Often the response a single man receives when he enters a single adult ministry will determine whether or not he returns. If the other men in the group treat him with suspicion or coolness, he may feel there is no place for him in your ministry. On the other hand, if the women respond by latching onto him and immediately asking him over to dinner or to social functions, he may also feel uncomfortable.

It's important to find the right balance in making single men feel comfortable, welcome, and free to participate at whatever level is appropriate for them.

One way to make a man feel welcome is to discover what his talents and gifts are and find a way he can use them in the ministry. This requires careful attention. I have often seen single men come to a ministry looking for a way to immediately get into leadership. For them, it becomes a way of reestablishing self-esteem, asserting control over their lives, getting attention, and continuing to do what they have done in the past. However, sometimes the very single men who seem so desperately interested in becoming involved are not actually ready to be in leadership positions. For example, a minister who has gone through a devastating divorce might go to a single adult ministry wanting to be reaffirmed as a minister. He may be hurt if he is not quickly involved and given a position of leadership that reflects his postion within the church.

One thing to look for is that sense of desperation and urgency. An effective leader is eager, willing, and ready but not usually desperate, hungry, and impatient. Of course, even someone who is not ready to assume the responsibilities and demands of leadership can still be a vital part of the ministry. He can still use his gifts and talents to some degree. Therefore, affirming the single men who come to you involves getting to know them, determining their gifts and abilities for involvement in your ministry, and making appropriate opportunities available for them to take a greater role in your ministry.

DEVELOP A MEN'S MINISTRY

Pray that God will give you one or more strong Christian men who have a vision for meeting the needs of other single men. Work with them to develop a ministry with men, by men. The design of this ministry will vary from group to group. Design yours to fit the needs and schedules of your own participants.

Some churches have well-developed discipleship programs where someone who has been through the formal discipleship program (a set number of weeks) takes on the mentor role and leads another person through the same formal program on a one-to-one basis.

Some churches have men's breakfasts once a month or even once a week. The focus is sometimes social and sometimes devotional. These regular meetings allow participants to get to know one another and develop Christian friendships over a period of time. Once a man has a friend, he is more likely to share problems on a personal basis.

Still other groups have a men's small-group program. It brings together groups of eight to 12 men on a regular basis, usually once a week, at a convenient time (often before work) for Bible study. They follow a chosen curriculum or systematic study of Scripture. Although the primary emphasis is on personal and spiritual growth, one of the side benefits is the development of male friendships.

Seminars on Saturdays "for men only" (with corresponding ones "for women only") are held by some groups. Retreats and men-only activities (deep-sea fishing, camping for the weekend, hunting, trail biking) are ideas used by other ministries.

However, as you design your ministry, remember the focus. Help men become comfortable attending your group and develop nonthreatening friendships with men. Make time available for them to interact with other men in social and developmental activities. Then you will have set the stage for an emotional openness when a need arises. When single men can become open with one another about personal issues, they are in a position to grow both personally and spiritually.

You will know you are successfully ministering with men when they come to your group, when they make a commitment to attend and to contribute, when your ministry challenges them spiritually and emotionally, and when you see life changes occurring. In the process, sometimes the number of single men attending your group will also increase, but this is not your goal.

CHECK YOUR MINISTRY WITH SINGLE MEN

✔ 1. What is the ratio of men to women in your ministry?

✔ 2. Do you provide sufficient physical activities?

✔ 3. Do you make single men feel welcome?

✔ 4. Do you have men in leadership positions?

✔ 5. Do you allow single men to become involved?

✔ 6. Have you deliberately planned a ministry with single men?

If these questions have helped you identify areas of your ministry in which you could improve, take action today!

chapter 14

CARE FOR SINGLE PARENTS AND THEIR CHILDREN

"I wouldn't trade my children for anything," one single mother commented wearily, "but I would like a day off!"

In your single adult ministry, there will be a significant number of single parents. Some will have custody, others will have joint custody, some will not have custody, and a few won't even have visitation rights. Single parents may never have married or be divorced, widowed, or long-term separated. Their children may be biological, adopted, or in some cases, step-children. Each type of parent has challenges that make their lives different and difficult.

The parent with custody has the pleasure of seeing their children daily, of participating in their daily growth and development, and the responsibility of providing the discipline and the care and guidance children need. The parent with custody may experience stress overload, financial problems, and emotional challenges. They need a little extra care and attention.

The parent without custody may be suffering from the loss of their children. As one dad said, "I wanted a divorce from my wife, not my children." These parents may have more freedom, but they may be more lonely because of the loss of daily contact with their children. They may feel guilty about not being there for their children. They may be angry if the relationship with the former spouse is not good and makes it difficult to spend time with their children.

Whatever the circumstances of the parents in your single adult ministry, you will want to be sensitive to their needs and design special ways to express the love of God to them.

Understand the Children

Many children born today will spend at least a part of their growing-up years in a single-parent home. Some researchers claim the figure to be as high as one in three. And a significant percentage of these will be children of divorced parents. The church has finally acknowledged that adults need assistance in getting through the pain of divorce and recovery and has responded with divorce recovery programs in most major cities. However, until recently, comparatively little was done for the children of divorced parents. Virtually all children assume some level of blame for the divorce of their parents. They believe if they had been better students, kept their rooms cleaner, stopped fighting with siblings, obeyed their parents more frequently, or caused less trouble, the divorce would never have occurred. Their guilt adds to their grief. They may attempt to effect reconciliations between their parents. Or they may push the parents into finding a new partner.

This self-imposed guilt causes children to keep asking over and over for "the real reason for the divorce." Regardless of how they phrase their questions, what they need is reassurance that:

• They did not cause the divorce.

• They are still loved by both parents, no matter how either is behaving.

• They will not be abandoned by the remaining parent.

In addition to the guilt, children usually experience many of the same emotions as their parents while they go through the grieving cycle: denial, bargaining, sadness, depression, anger, powerlessness, a sense of rejection, abandonment, and isolation. They may respond by withdrawing, regressing to an earlier childhood stage, striking back with aggression, failing in school, giving up on themselves, losing interest in everything, experiencing moodiness, lethargy, having physical pain and illness, or becoming increasingly demanding of physical contact (hugging, holding, clinging).

When there is a trauma such as a divorce, children may also change what they believe in these six areas: concept of self, parents, God, marriage, life, and what is right and wrong.

Their concept of self may change when they feel responsible for the divorce and experience powerlessness to make things okay again. Their concept of parents changes because instead of looking up to them as wise and strong, they now are angry with one or both and blame one or both for not being able to make the marriage work. Their concept of God may change as they begin to question how a loving God would allow such pain to happen and why God doesn't answer their prayers in such an important matter. They take a look at marriage and often make one of two promises: "I'll never get a divorce no matter what!" or "I'll never get married." Their concept of life now includes "Life isn't fair." And often they begin to believe that they don't have to keep their promises because their parents didn't keep their wedding vows.

Ministering to children of divorced parents includes becoming aware of the serious issues these children face and the strong emotions they experience. It means reaching out in love to ease the pain and help them through. These children should be integrated into the Christian education program, but they also need a period of extra support for recovery. Leaders assigned to work with the children need not be professionals in child development or child psychology, but they do need to know how to relate to children.

WAYS TO CARE

Here are several ways to reach out in love to single parents:

Provide respite

The 24-hour-a-day responsibility of being a single parent weighs heavily on most people. When the children are small, even going to the grocery store at the last minute for a loaf of bread can be a major undertaking if the day has been stressful and the children are cranky. When children are sick, there is no one else to take a turn at being a patient nurse. When teenagers are rebellious, there is no partner to help hold the line on house rules.

Giving a single parent an afternoon, an evening, or a weekend of freedom can be the best gift in the world. It is amazing just how rejuvenated a parent will feel within only a few hours. Their attitude can change from hopeless to hopeful. Their perspective can turn from this-is-the-end-of-the-world to this-is-just-one-more-little-problem. Respite can be provided by other single parents, teenagers, single adults with no children, older adults, married couples, or through the church day care center.

What single parents do with their time alone will vary: sleep, clean house, read, shop, go to the beach, go out to dinner, spend time with friends, sit alone in a quiet house, or take a warm bath. Just knowing that they will have an afternoon or evening once a month, or a weekend once a quarter, to be alone and do whatever they wish will keep many single parents going.

Provide child care at events

Be sure to provide child care at each of your functions and meetings. People who need your ministry the most may not be able to attend your activities because they can't afford child care. Pay for child care by charging a little extra for a function. (As little as 50 cents extra per person can net $20 if 40 people attend.) You also can collect an offering for child care or pay for the child care out of your budget or treasury.

Provide education

Seminars on single parenting are often well-attended because parents want to know what they are doing wrong. They want advice on coping and functioning as single parents. Key issues involve discipline, teaching values, dealing with former spouses, helping children get over anger, and finding ways to deal with practical problems.

Help parents understand that their job is to communicate values, model them, encourage children to interact about applying the values in different situations, set standards in the home, and consistently apply the consequences of breaking the rules. Children have the option whether or not to accept the values and take ownership for themselves. Parents do not get to choose which values their children finally "buy" for themselves. Parents often feel guilty if children do not choose the same values they themselves hold.

One way to help single parents is to provide books in the church (or single adult ministry) library on parenting and coping as a single parent.

Provide opposite-sex role models

Single mothers raising sons frequently complain that they wish there were Christian men who could provide male role models for their boys. (Single fathers raising daughters usually say they have little difficulty finding women who want to serve as role models for their girls.) Single parents and their children often respond to Christian Big Brother and Big Sister programs. This type of program is one of the best ways to care for single parents, although it is not easy to coordinate and maintain.

Big Brothers and Big Sisters spend time with the children on activities or projects such as hiking, playing tennis, bowling, making crafts, or just everyday activities such as cooking, cleaning the garage, grocery shopping, washing the car, or sewing. The program emphasizes caring for the child and teaching the skills that children need for living in an adult world.

Another option: Married families might "adopt" a single-parent family and include them, or at least the children, in family outings. In this way, a father spending time with his boys can also provide help to a boy from a single-parent family. Or a mother spending time with her daughters can share herself with a girl from a single-parent family.

Including male teachers as well as women in the children and youth department of Sunday school and weekday programs is another way the church can reach out with role models to children of divorced parents. In this way, other Christians have the opportunity to share the emotional burden of child rearing with the single parent. It provides mother/father image relationships. Some parents do not have contact with their own children. The contact with other people's children may help heal their wounds.

Provide practical assistance

Many single adult ministries provide practical help to single parents.

- *Recycled Christmas* is a program in one church where parents (married and single) bring in toys their children have outgrown or no longer use. Single parents choose a toy for each of their children as a Christmas present. In this way, Christmas expenses are reduced.

- *Clothing exchange* includes a children's "clothes closet." Parents (married and single) bring outgrown clothing that has been laundered, mended, and marked with the sizes. Single parents "shop" for the free clothing.

- *Furniture exchange* can be coordinated by posting on a bulletin board what is needed and what is available from single adults and couples in the church. If telephone numbers are posted along with the other information, individuals can make their own arrangements for pickup or delivery.

- *Service coupons* was an idea that caught on in one large church. Professionals within the church donated services to single parents. The minister/leader solicited the services and based on the "donations" made coupons that entitled the bearer to a free dental checkup, a set of x-rays, a car tune up, an oil change, a haircut, a chiropractic adjustment, etc. These coupons were given to single parents when those needs were expressed.

Provide support groups

Single parents often want and benefit by having a weekly, or at least monthly, support group where they can come together and share. As one mother put it, "It feels so good to hear the other single parents sharing. I used to think I was the only one who felt the way I do about being a single mom. Now I know my frustrations are normal. It's easier to cope."

Children need a recovery group for a few weeks also. This can be held at the same time as a divorce recovery class for adults. Curriculum available to help you design these support groups is found in Appendix B.

Be sensitive

Children of single-parent families may alternate between homes and be unable to attend Sunday school (or weekday programs) every week. Therefore, your church will want to be careful when planning attendance or memory verse contests that require weekly attendance.

Single parents and children of single-parent families may not be able to participate in Mother-Daughter or Father-Son activities if they don't live with the designated parent. Therefore, your church may want to rethink planning such activities or changing the designations.

Single parents and children of single-parent families may have difficulty with certain holidays such as Mothers' Day or Fathers' Day. Be careful how you handle activities (such as making a card for Dad).

Single parents need group activities where it is acceptable to bring their children. Therefore, when planning the calendar for your single adult ministry, be sure to include some activities for single adults only and some that invite single parents to bring their children.

Some churches have strict rules about who can pick up younger children from their classes. Teachers need to be aware that in some single-parent families, the arrangements are that one parent drops off the children and the other one picks up the children. You will want to make arrangements to avoid problems if children are transferred in this way.

Your single adult ministry is incomplete until you have an effective and caring ministry with single parents and their children.

CHECK YOUR MINISTRY WITH SINGLE PARENTS AND THEIR CHILDREN

✔ 1. Do you provide respite?

✔ 2. Do you provide child care?

✔ 3. Do you provide educational opportunities?

✔ 4. Do you provide practical support and assistance?

✔ 5. Do you provide opposite-sex role models?

✔ 6. Is your program and church sensitive to single parents?

If these questions have helped you identify areas in which your single adult ministry could be improved, take action today!

chapter 15

RESPOND WITH RECOVERY PROGRAMS

"This is my third time through the Divorce Recovery Workshop," Kurt admitted cheerfully. "First I went through as a participant, and this is my second time serving as one of the small-group facilitators."

Recovery is a process. You don't suddenly wake up one morning and say, "I've decided I'm going to recover from a major life trauma/problem," and it is done! Although a person can recover from a trauma or problem on his or her own, the healing can be speeded up and be more effective through group process. Many churches have become very successful at divorce recovery and grief recovery through their single adult ministry.

Larger churches, or churches where the membership indicated a specific need, have also opened their doors to a variety of support groups. These include Alcoholics Anonymous, Narcotics Anonymous, Al-Anon, and other groups that provide recovery programs for sexual addictions, eating disorders, compulsive behaviors, abuse, and adult children of ...

Check your local bookstores or contact local chapters of recovery organizations for literature helpful in designing an effective recovery program.

"TWELVE STEP" PROGRAMS

Many of the recovery programs use the "twelve step" approach popularized by Alcoholics Anonymous and proven effective by thousands of people. Basically an adaptation of the twelve step process would include:

1. Admitting an addiction and one's powerlessness to control it.

2. Acknowledging that God's forgiveness and care can help overcome addictions.

3. Asking the Holy Spirit's guidance in submitting one's life to God.

4. Conducting an honest, moral appraisal of one's self.

5. Confessing to God and another person the extent of one's failings.

6. Becoming willing for God to remove the defects of one's character.

7. Asking that God remove those defects.

8. Listing everyone whom a person has harmed and being willing to make amends to each one.

9. Making amends to each person who has been offended or harmed whenever possible.

10. Continually evaluating one's life and immediately acknowledging when one is wrong.

11. Seeking to increase in the knowledge of God through prayer and meditation.

12. Reaching out to others to assist them in recovery and using these principles in all areas of life.

Different programs adapt these steps to fit the problem being addressed and vary the time involved in the recovery support-group process. Some start a new group and run it for 12 weeks, focusing one week on each step. In those cases, the group is usually closed to new participants after the second session so that everyone in the group has the same information. In other cases, people enter and leave the group at different times, and participants progress through the steps at their own rates.

The first approach is more therapeutically sound because there is a building block effect. What one learns one week builds on what was covered the previous week. Also, participants seem more committed to staying together through the process of regaining control. However, it is true that everyone does progress at an individual rate. Just because a person attends a 12-week support group does not mean that the recovery is complete and guaranteed.

If you are interested in beginning support groups using the twelve step program, your local secular (as well as Christian) bookstore will provide you with several helpful books. See Appendix B.

DIVORCE AND GRIEF RECOVERY

The recovery or support-group process to assist people through recuperation from a divorce or death of a spouse may use the twelve step approach. More often than not, it follows the grief recovery cycle and focuses on one step each week. Usually, weekly sessions are topical rather than process oriented. The grief cycle as explained by Elisabeth Kübler-Ross and modified by various practitioners includes:

1. Shock

   A person's first response to divorce or the death of a spouse is usually shock. The physiological reaction to emotional shock is often numbness or severe pain.

2. Denial

Immediately following shock comes denial. "This can't be happening to me!" the person asserts. Some people keep up with daily routines in an effort to ignore the reality.

3. Bargaining

When a person acknowledges that perhaps the spouse truly is serious about getting a divorce, there is a bargaining period. "I'll do anything! Just stay and don't leave!" "I'll change!" "I'm sorry; I didn't realize!"

When a spouse dies the survivor may attempt to bargain with God. "Please don't let this nightmare be real."

4. Depression

As a person accepts the reality of the loss, anger is directed toward the self. "If only I had been a better spouse!" "I should have treated my spouse better." "It's all my fault." Assuming the blame for either the death or the divorce causes a person to be very angry, sad, and depressed.

5. Anger

Finally, a person reaches a point of honesty. He or she acknowledges some degree of fault on both sides. As part of the healing process, the depression begins to lift, and the anger is directed outward. "I was wrong, but so was my spouse! How could that person treat me this way?" "Maybe I didn't always say and do the right things, but my spouse is also to blame for the fatal accident because he/she didn't use the seat belt!"

6. Forgiveness

When anger is acknowledged, faults can be confessed and forgiven. Without forgiveness, there will be no lasting healing. When one has been hurt, no amount of restitution, loving behavior, or time will exorcise the hurt, although its effect can lessen. Only forgiveness can take the pain out of hurt. Only forgiveness opens the door for healing.

7. Acceptance

There comes a time when the individual accepts reality and adopts a new lifestyle. Being single again may still be scary, may still be undesirable. When a person accepts reality, he or she is no longer a victim and can once again take charge of life and begin making positive choices.

8. Hope

Learning to laugh again, to plan for a future, to build new friendships and even risk a new romance are evidence of hope renewed. With new hope, a person is truly ready to move forward with confidence and reach out with compassion toward others in the recovery process.

However, a person need not have completed the grieving process to reach out to others with comfort and caring concern. A person can still be struggling with a few leftover issues of forgiveness and be effective as a group facilitator as long as a person is honest with self and others.

Some divorce and grief recovery programs begin on a Friday evening and continue all day Saturday. Other churches find that a once-a-week evening meeting works best. Sessions last about an hour and a half and continue for eight to 10 weeks. In this format, participants can put principles into practice on a weekly basis. The two- or three-month time period also gives participants time to see progress in their healing. In this effective model, the leader provides refreshments at the beginning, allows a few moments of casual fellowship, gives a minilecture on the topic/step of the evening, and then divides the group into small-group discussions with facilitators who keep the discussions on track. Facilitators usually have gone through the divorce recovery program themselves. The evening ends with prayer.

The following chart compares a ministry with the widowed to a ministry with the divorced.

Comparison of Ministry with the Widowed and the Divorced

This chart was compiled after interviews with pastors, counselors, widowed persons, divorced persons, and after completing the reading for this project, as well as 19 years of personal experience in the field of single adult ministry.

Ministry with the Widowed

1. Best led by a person who has been widowed, or if necessary, someone who is very sensitive to the needs/challenges of the widowed.

2. Needs to provide small-group interaction during the initial support-group sessions.

3. Best format is to have support groups that meet weekly for several weeks.

4. Initial support-group period needs to be limited to six to 12 weeks. Follow-up ministry may continue for several weeks.

5. Needs to encourage members to talk about the deceased and the good times they had and the good memories. Mentioning the deceased's name is an important need of the widowed.

6. Don't push members to let go of possessions, photos, and other mementos too quickly.

7. Needs to deal with forgiveness.

8. Needs to focus on taking charge of present situations, necessary life decisions, and positive self talk.

9. Must encourage the widowed to regain control of life by setting up a structure, keeping a schedule, following through on plans, and taking care of self.

Ministry with the Divorced

1. Best led by a person who has been divorced, or if necessary, someone who is very sensitive to the needs/challenges of the divorced.

2. Needs to provide small-group interaction during the initial support-group sessions.

3. Best format is to have support groups that meet weekly for several weeks.

4. Initial support-group period needs to be limited to six to 12 weeks. Follow-up ministry may continue for several weeks.

5. Needs to encourage members to talk about their present situations and not dwell on the past and the pain.

6. Needs to assist members in letting go of past painful memories and possessions early in the recovery process.

7. Needs to deal with forgiveness.

8. Needs to focus on taking charge of present situations, necessary life decisions, and positive self talk.

9. Must encourage the divorced to regain control of life by setting up a structure, keeping a schedule, following through on plans, taking care of self, reclaiming areas of one's world, and avoiding encounters with the former spouse.

10. Should help the widowed restructure basic assumptions about life and faith to cope with getting on with life after the loss.

11. Don't lump widowed adults with divorced adults because they aren't "bitter" about their former spouses. Sometimes, after the initial recovery period, the widowed are willing to be part of a general single adult ministry.

12. Single-parenting issues may need to be addressed.

13. Sexuality issues need to be a part of the long-term ministry with the widowed.

14. Remarriage may be addressed in the long-term ministry but not in the initial support-group curriculum.

10. Should help the divorced restructure basic assumptions about life and faith to cope with getting on with life after the divorce.

11. Don't mind if widowed or never-married single adults join in shared general ministry, although separate support groups for the divorced are appropriate.

12. Single-parenting issues may need to be addressed.

13. Sexuality issues need to be a part of the long-term ministry with the divorced.

14. Remarriage may be addressed in the long-term ministry but not in the initial support-group curriculum.

NETWORK

Avoid being exclusive or territorial in providing support or recovery programs. Even if you believe that you have designed the best program there could be, don't hesitate to refer someone to another program if the needs are immediate and your program or group cannot meet the need.

In some cities, churches will take turns hosting various recovery programs. In others, churches will specialize and divide up the various programs among themselves. Unfortunately, in some areas, there is still a sense of competition. This means that a person might call for help with a painful divorce and be told that the current group is closed to new participants and the next group starts in six months. What is the hurting person supposed to do in the meantime?

Don't let that happen to a single adult who contacts your ministry for assistance.

CHECK YOUR RECOVERY PROGRAMS

✔ 1. Do you at least provide divorce and grief recovery programs at your church?

✔ 2. Do you provide other recovery programs?

✔ 3. Do you have a list of recovery programs, meeting times, and session starting dates available in your city to use as a referral list?

✔ 4. Do you have a good curriculum?

✔ 5. Do you provide a table of helpful books at each session?

If these questions have helped you identify areas in which you could improve your ministry, take action today!

chapter 16

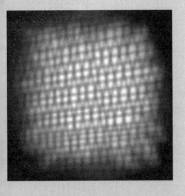

ENCOURAGE COMMITMENT TO MISSIONS

Larry was different when he came back from a short-term mission trip to Central America. He seemed to have a different perspective on life, on priorities, on what was important, and on his own Christian walk. Already he was talking of going back.

Encouraging your single adults to make a commitment to missions can be one of the more significant things you can do to help them grow spiritually. Jesus left His disciples with a commandment to go into all the world in His name, preaching and teaching people about the Gospel (Matt. 28:19–20). Even as He prepared to ascend into heaven, He promised that the disciples would receive the Holy Spirit's power. Jesus commissioned them as witnesses for Him, not only at home in Jerusalem, but in all Judea, in Samaria, and to the uttermost parts of the earth (Acts 1:8). But even earlier in His ministry, Jesus sent disciples out on "practice" mission trips. They came back excited as they shared what had happened (Luke 9:1–10).

As Christians entrusted with the Good News of the Gospel of Jesus Christ, we are challenged to share that Good News with our world. Sharing means not only telling what great things God has done in our lives, but also loving others in the Lord's name. Christians love in deed as well as words (1 John 3:18). Through mission projects and trips, your single adults can do both.

BENEFITS OF SHORT-TERM MISSION TRIPS

A short-term mission trip is usually designed to benefit a missionary, a local church, or a Christian project such as an orphanage, a school, or a camp, either in the United States or abroad. A team of single adults gather together the necessary resources, skilled people, and finances to complete an identified project, which can usually be completed in one or two weeks. The accommodations for the team range from none (bring your sleeping bag, water purification tablets, and canteens) to primitive (sleep at the camp or school).

The true benefit of a short-term mission trip, especially when you travel to a poor community or country, is the change in your single adults. They will never be the same again. Chris Eaton, founder of Bridge Builders (an organization that assists groups in planning, organizing, and executing short-term mission trips), gives several reasons a single adult ministry leader would want to consider planning a mission trip.

We are commanded to be missionaries

Even if your single adults cannot or will not devote their lives to being full-time missionaries, they can participate in one or more short-term mission trips or projects. Christians need the opportunity to share the Gospel (both in words and in actions) during their lifetime.

Single adults experience God in a unique way

Outside familiar surroundings, facing physical dangers, single adults often experience a different relationship with God. In Third World countries whose governments are unstable, where wars and violence are common, or where wild animals or unfamiliar germs can attack, singles realize what it means to rely on God and draw closer to Him. Most single adults returning from a short-term mission trip relate that the experience has brought them closer to an understanding of God and the need to reach out to others in our world.

Single adults get back more than they give

Your single adults will return convinced they received more than they gave. What each one receives varies, but virtually everyone comes back feeling enriched, humbled by the knowledge that in middle-class America we have so much more than most of the rest of the world.

The mission team will bond together

Single adults who go together on a short-term mission trip tend to form an intimate, lasting bond. There is something about sharing the rigors of the jungle, the memories of the problems, the joys of the experience, and the spiritual insights that minimizes individual differences and forges a sense of team spirit. People find ways to communicate, relate, and reach out to one another that transcend past petty conflicts.

Single adults on short-term mission trips meet needs

Adding a new classroom, putting on a new roof, painting buildings, landscaping a camp, building a church, making shelves, sewing curtains—these needs can be met by your single adults on a short-term mission trip. Without the mission team, they would not get done. Other projects are too costly for a missionary or local church to afford without outside help (buildings, landscaping, plumbing).

Single adults, excited about a project, can often raise unbelievable sums of money from their communities to support mission projects. They might not only raise funds but also recruit experts (carpenters, electricians, plumbers) who go along and help. Often, groups find doctors and nurses to join the team.

Single adults experience miracles

In remote locations where there are few resources, one tends to be more dependent on God. And God is faithful. Therefore, single adults who go on short-term mission trips often are privileged to experience firsthand miracles they will never forget. They see God's hand of protection, rescue, and intervention. They pray together and receive dramatic answers. They hear stories from the local people or the missionary about the faithfulness of God during times of need. In the process, single adults grow in faith.

Single adults learn about their world

Sometimes single adults give little thought to a country or the people who live there. Experiencing a week or two of living in a foreign place heightens their awareness and kindles their interest, both practically and spiritually. They become more sensitive to the needs of the country. They pray intelligently in the future when they hear news reports about the country they visited.

Single adults become aware of needs in their own cities

Your single adults will come to realize that they don't have to leave home to find a mission field, needy people, or work they can do for the Lord. There are poor communities, churches, and people in all of our cities. There are needs right next door that the people of God can and should meet.

Often single adults return from a mission trip with a new vision for reaching out to their own communities and immediately become involved in local projects.

IDENTIFYING A PROJECT

There are several ways to find prospective countries for short-term mission trips and identify a project your single adults might want to undertake.

Write to the missionaries your church supports

Most churches support missionaries in foreign countries as well as in the United States and Canada. Write a letter to them asking about the feasibility of bringing 10 or more of your single adults to visit and do a project. Ask what types of projects would be needed and appropriate for your group to consider.

Contact missionary organizations

There are several large missionary organizations you may contact. They may suggest ideas about possible locations and projects. Possibly they will send a representative to your single adult group to speak and present the challenge and the project.

Contact Bridge Builders

Write Chris Eaton at Bridge Builders, 9925 7th Way N., #102, St. Petersburg, FL 33702.

Contact your denominational headquarters

Your denominational headquarters may have information about projects needed by denominational missionaries.

Contact other single adult ministers/leaders who have taken short-term mission trips

One of your best sources of information will be other ministers/leaders of single adult ministries who have taken trips with their groups. They can give helpful tips and help you avoid mistakes they may have made.

After you contact these sources, review their responses and consider the cost of each possibility, both in terms of the transportation for the team as well as the cost of the project itself. You may want to start small so your first project will be a success. Do something in the United States, perhaps some-place you can drive to (far enough away to be interesting, at least out of state) and plan a three- or four-day project.

One group in California adopted an orphanage just across the border in Mexico. Several single adults pile into a van and go to the orphanage about twice a year. They do repairs, bring toys and clothes for the children, work in the yard, read to the children, play games, hold and love the babies, cut hair, and mend clothing while they are there. The group talked with local hotels who were glad to donate used sheets and pillow cases that seemed like new to the orphans in Mexico.

One group chose a project at an out-of-state school and spent several days working on finishing and painting the walls of a new classroom. This saved the school many dollars.

You can start with the skills you know you have within your group and choose a project, or you can choose a project and go out recruiting people with the skills you need. Either approach works, but the latter tends to increase the level of participation you have from single adults. People like to be needed, and when someone is told that his or her skills are needed for an important project, he or she often agrees to participate if possible.

TEAM PREPARATION

Once you select a location and project, get your team ready. Don't forget to:
❑ Find out about the country.

Assign different team members to find out all they can about the country and location. They can go to the library, government agencies, con-sulates, or write to the local church or missionary you will be visiting. Have information sessions where team members present what they have learned. If possible, get slides, films, or other photographs to help team members visualize what they will be facing.

❏ Find out what is needed to get into the country.

Check with government agencies, travel agencies, and the consulates of the country you will be visiting to discover what identification or permissions (passports, visas) are needed and what inoculations are required or desirable. Identify the procedures for obtaining these.

❏ Make lists of what to take.

Discover what is needed (mosquito netting, sleeping bags, insect repellent, water purification tablets, canteens, dried or canned foods, types of clothing and shoes, hats, etc.). Help people make wise decisions about what to take and how to pack in case transportation space is limited or they have to walk and carry their gear.

An important consideration is food. If food is provided by the local people or missionary, then you will need to take very little except for snacks, possibly American coffee, and special items such as artificial sweeteners. If you provide your own, carefully plan meals that use dried, canned, or packaged foods.

❏ Set up an organizational structure.

Designate a leader and an assistant leader. In some cases, identify the roles of each team member before they leave home. Even though everyone is expected to pitch in where needed, it is important that there is a designated leader.

❏ Build a team before you leave.

Build the team identity. Have the team meet several times before they leave to pray together, plan, study God's Word, the logistics, and the project. Give everyone a chance to work together and resolve minor differences before they are away from home.

❏ Give the team a send off.

When the team is ready to leave, make it a celebration. Invite all of your single adults to come and pray with the team, rejoice together, and affirm the team in their project. Those who can't go can still feel a part of the project by giving money to help with costs, by promising to be a prayer partner, or by coming to encourage the team as they leave. The team is a representative of the entire group.

DON'T FORGET TO FOLLOW UP!

As soon as possible after the team returns, gather everyone together and have the team report to the entire group about the success of the project. Encourage them to tell everything, the fun, the misery, the joys and the struggles, the unexpected and the predictable, the miracles, the disappointments, and what they learned through the project. Then piggyback on the enthusiasm. Either enlist a group for the next trip or begin considering projects you can do in your own city.

• Are there homeless people? You can gather personal grooming supplies and pack small paper bags with shampoo, soap, combs, sewing kits, razors, bags of laundry soap, and any number of similar items. Take these to the homeless or to shelters for distribution.

- Check out centers that provide meals to the homeless. Sign up to bag food or serve dinners.

- Collect sleeping bags, blankets, or coats for the homeless and take them to shelters for distribution.

- Consider a project to help the elderly in your church. Prepare meals, clean yards, do housework, or run errands.

- What about starting a tutoring center after school for latchkey children who have no parents at home until after working hours?

- Consider a volunteer literacy program for your community.

The ideas are unlimited; the needs are unending. The possibilities are there. Use your creativity. Ask God to show you what you can do to further the Gospel by being an ambassador of good will and love to your community. Involve your single adults in missions, at home and abroad.

CHECK YOUR MISSION INVOLVEMENT

✔ 1. Have you presented the idea of a mission trip/project to your group?

✔ 2. Have you ever participated in a short-term mission project yourself?

✔ 3. Have you researched possibilities of trips/projects for your single adults?

✔ 4. What ways does your group reach out to those in need right in your city?

If these questions have identified ways in which you can make your single adult ministry better, take action today!

chapter 17

CONSIDER SPECIAL SINGLE ADULTS

Paula needs lots of attention. As soon as someone notices her or speaks to her in a friendly way, Paula latches on and monopolizes that person, believing she has found a new best friend. She will telephone the "friend" several times an evening. In groups, Paula will interrupt other conversations, demanding attention. Most people have learned to avoid or turn away from Paula, even though they feel they are being rude.

Roger has Down's Syndrome. He hugs people as a way of making contact. He is very polite but very friendly. Roger greets everyone who comes to the single adult ministry at his church by standing at the door and trying to hug them. Then he circulates around the room, trying to get hugs all evening.

Sally Ann lives on the street. She has no home. Everything she owns is stored in a shopping cart that she pushes everywhere she goes. Every so often, she finds a way of taking a shower and cleaning up. She has discovered a single adult ministry at a church she can walk to from the park where she sleeps. She comes to all the activities held at the church. Sally Ann doesn't want to get a job or have a permanent home. She claims she is perfectly happy living as a "homeless" individual. She is not on the same wavelength as the rest of the participants, which causes awkward silences or spirited debates. Sally Ann also has a body odor problem.

Mark is a local single-again stockbroker. He hops from one single adult group to another. Mark is attractive, dresses well, and makes a terrific first impression. However, he preys on vulnerable women, enticing them into emotional and sexual commitments and borrowing money from them. Then he leaves them heartbroken and emotionally destroyed.

Cynthia is a headstrong manager. She takes charge at work, at home, and tries to take over any activity, meeting, conversation, or relationship

127

in which she has a part. Cynthia has a deep-seated anger toward men that began as a child when her father beat her and her mother. It progressed when she was hurt by a teenage boyfriend, continued with a destructive relationship with her husband, and deepened when she experienced a bitter divorce. That anger underlies all her communication and her relationships. Cynthia steamrolls over people, putting them off, and sometimes driving them away.

You may have a Paula, Roger, Sally Ann, Mark, or Cynthia in your single adult ministry. What do you do?

REMEMBER YOUR MISSION

Remember that the primary mission of a single adult ministry is to reach out and assist single adults to build or rebuild healthy, productive, personal and spiritual lives. As such, your ministry is basically with healthy persons who may be experiencing a temporary period of emotional or spiritual imbalance or be stuck developmentally at some point.

While you provide counseling, you are not a counseling service for serious problems. These get referred to a professional counselor or center. If you, or one of your leaders, is a trained Christian counselor and provides counseling to the seriously disturbed or dysfunctional person, that counseling is adjunct to, and not necessarily an integral part of, your single adult ministry.

While you provide a safe place for persons who are temporarily struggling, hurting, or broken, you are not a dumping place for anyone who is not married, regardless of the other problems they may have. Therefore, the needs of the group cannot be sacrificed to the needs of one individual. A wise leader will protect the group from continued disruption by one or two individuals. Therefore, first identify the problem behaviors and attempt to work with the individuals to eliminate the problems. If you are still unsuccessful, the disruptive individual can be excluded from attending group activities and meetings.

REMEMBER TO CARE

The single adult ministry is not the place for disruptive persons, but this does not mean they are to be excluded from love, care, or attention. In as much as we do something to one of the least of God's children, we are doing it to the Lord Himself. Therefore, give an individual every chance to learn to participate in an appropriate manner within the group before excluding that person from participation. If exclusion is absolutely necessary, then choose alternate ways of caring and ministering with the person.

You can care for the mentally challenged by referring them for counseling through your church, local social service agencies, or a Christian counseling center. As a loving outreach, your group may even take on the financial responsibility of paying for the counseling fees.

You can care for the developmentally challenged by being understanding and caring for them on an individual basis. One or two single adults can commit to spending time with such individuals (if they truly can't attend functions without being disruptive).

You can care for the homeless by providing warm clothes, blankets, sleeping bags, toiletries, and shelter options. Help them find a way to bathe and at least eat one meal a day. Homeless people might be welcomed at the weekly family dinners sponsored by your church where there is no organized activity other than eating and fellowshiping. They would not be that disruptive in such a setting.

You can care for a person (male or female) who is a sexual scalp hunter by getting a mature Christian of the same sex to befriend the person and spend time helping that person learn how destructive such behavior is, not only to a group, but also to both parties involved.

You can care for those who are aggressive, angry, or bitter by befriending them, helping them learn to trust, and perhaps by recommending counselling.

As you can see, caring for disruptive individuals is not a function of the single adult ministry as a whole, but it is a response to the commandment to love one another and care for each other as part of the body of Christ. It's true that you cannot successfully love and care for each person who visits your ministry. But it is important that you and your leaders develop ways to reach out, even to those for whom ministry as a whole is inappropriate.

When the problems of specific disruptive people are beyond your expertise, refer them to the appropriate professionals. Sometimes this means the church leaders. Sometimes professional counselors. And regrettably, sometimes the police, as in the case of fraud, abuse, peeping Toms/Janes, or other cases where the law is being broken.

CHECK YOUR READINESS FOR THE SPECIAL SINGLE ADULT

✔ 1. Do you have a list of resources to which special people can be referred?

✔ 2. Have you developed a personal contact with these resources so you can make a personal or an urgent referral?

✔ 3. Have you and your leaders discussed how to deal with special single adults?

✔ 4. Have you and your leaders successfully dealt with special single adults?

✔ 5. Have you learned how to be gentle but firm, caring but insistent, and able to exclude from the group individuals who are, at least for now, unable to participate in a productive manner?

✔ 6. Do you have in place ways to reach out in love to special individuals without sacrificing the needs of the group?

If these questions have helped you identify areas in which you could improve your ministry, take action today!

chapter 18

CHANGE AS THE NEED ARISES

Marlene walked into the single adult Sunday school class for the first time in four weeks. She had been in the hospital for surgery and because of complications, she had not been able to come to church until now. The class seemed different somehow. There were many people present she did not recognize. They were following a different format for the class. For just a few minutes, Marlene felt out of place, then a couple of close friends spied her and came over with warm hugs and even warmer greetings. She was home after all.

Any living organism continually changes. Sometimes the change is slow and almost impossible to see. At other times, growth is dynamic and impossible to ignore. Your single adult ministry is a living organism as well as an organization, and it must be sensitive and responsive to the changing needs of your adults. You can't just organize a ministry, set it in motion, and forget it. The best program in the world today may not meet the needs of tomorrow's world because the people in your group are also in the process of changing. Newly divorced persons who walk into your group today need a whole different kind of ministry than they will need a year from now. With the recovery period passed, they will have a new perspective.

Transiency among single adult groups requires change. Single adults come and go with more freedom than most married people. They can, and do, move, change jobs, or start attending another church. Some will marry and move on. If you checked the membership rosters of your group every six months, an average of about half of the names would be new. And as new people come to your group, they bring their own sets of expectations, backgrounds, and needs.

Watch for Signals

Most of the time you'll be able to tell when program changes are necessary. Problems signal the need for modifications. Here are a few such problems.

Nonattendance

Has the attendance at one of your regular activities dropped off recently without a specific reason? Are just the same few people faithfully there each week? Perhaps the activities are not suited to the interests of the group. Maybe there are personality conflicts and grudges between some of the members that need to be resolved in a spirit of love.

Disinterest

Do your single adults just go along with whatever is planned without offering suggestions or getting excited? Is the group in a rut, doing the same activities month after month? Perhaps your people are bored! This disinterest can spring from a lack of involvement in the planning processes or from a lack of motivation to participate. Try to stimulate interest by including as many single adults as possible in making decisions about which monthly functions are scheduled. Include them in the planning process.

Same leaders

Are the same few people elected to office term after term? Sometimes the same people remain in office just because no one else cares enough to get involved. This doesn't give others an opportunity to serve and grow. Also leaders can grow weary and lose their creativity after serving several terms. New leaders can bring new energy and ideas to your group.

Complaints

Complainers, who believe nothing is ever done correctly, appear in every ministry. You'll want to learn to listen to, but not take too seriously, the negative feedback from these sources. On the other hand, if you hear complaints from several sources regarding something in the program, chances are you need to investigate further and make some changes.

No growth

Maybe your attendance hasn't dropped off, but neither has it grown. Members don't bring in new people, and visitors don't often return. Sometimes this occurs because the group has been together long enough so that they know each other too well. There is an underlying friendship within the group that automatically, although unintentionally, makes a visitor feel left out. Challenge your single adults to reach out and share the love of Christ with others. Involve the group in planning outreach activities.

Rapid growth

If your single adult ministry is rapidly growing in numbers, you're obviously doing something right! But you'll have to be prepared to modify your ministry to cope with rapid growth.

- You may need more meeting space.

- You may need more leaders.

- You may need more organization (i.e. policies, procedures, people, forms, supplies).

- You may need to refine your ministry by providing activities for special-interest groups within the program.

- You may have to divide the group into smaller classes or subgroups.

  Be ready to change as the need arises.

BE FLEXIBLE WHEN CREATING A NEW CLASS OR SUBGROUP

Once your single adult ministry has a membership of more than 50 or 60 in regular attendance, you will probably be faced with the issue of grouping your members into more than one class or subgroup. You may consider several options. Select the best method for your group.

The first alternative is grouping by age levels. For most adult classes, this method is quite appropriate because people at similar age levels are usually experiencing similar life choices, problems, and personal victories. This is because normal adult development roughly corresponds to chronological age. Young adults are in the process of breaking away from their primary families and establishing their own identities. Adults in their 30s and 40s are often raising adolescent children, experiencing a reflective period, and sometimes making major life changes. Older people face retirement, the loss of family and friends, and have time to explore interests long since shelved in place of raising families and earning a living.

Having similar challenges and problems provides a basis for interaction and acceptance of one another. Hence age groups are usually successful for adults.

There are a few problems, however, in arbitrarily using age groups for your single adult ministry.

- During periods of special crisis such as divorce or losing a spouse by death, normal stages of adult development are suspended. The most important issue becomes adjustment to the loss of a spouse, a relationship, an identity, and a whole new lifestyle.

- A person who is suddenly single again tends to be facing a situation similar to that faced by people in their 20s—the challenge of establishing one's self again in the world. This makes the age difference irrelevant.

- The thought of growing "old" is more frightening to single adults who wonder if they will ever again find a life companion. Asking single adults to go into an "over 40s" class with contented married couples their own age can trigger a rebellion based on this deep, sometimes unacknowledged, fear.

- Sometimes the youthful exuberance and "bounceability" of the younger single adults can motivate older adults to accept their new, single-again status. The wisdom and experienced maturity of older adults can also have a positive influence on the younger single adults.

Exercise some flexibility when planning how to divide your single adults into small groups. One minister shared his story.

When his single adult ministry was first formed (with more than 100 members), classes were divided by age groups. There were four classes. The 20s, the 30s, the 40–50s, and the over-50s. After several years, only the 30s class was actually viable. A careful analysis of the situation showed that the 30s class was so popular that the more active and involved people from the other classes began attending it. This, of course, took strength away from the other classes, and now they were faltering.

Trying to realign the classes again almost threatened the entire ministry. People who were asked to go to their own classes felt rejected and offended. Only after much prayer and careful, and sometimes tearful, planning, could they reach a compromise. The age divisions would have a period of overlap. This allowed some flexibility so people could be in the class of their choice and have time to develop a relationship in the next class they would move into. So the classes became the 20–35s, the 30–45s, the 40–65s, and the over-60s. At least once a quarter, there would be an activity (picnic or party) planned for all the classes. Slowly the wounds healed, and the groups became effective once again.

Take note and be careful not to become too legalistic with your rules. Don't make people "prove" that they are in the correct class. Remember, it is better to have single adults in a "wrong class" than not to have them attend at all!

WHAT TO DO WITH YOUR ALUMNI

Another area where some leaders tend to become legalistic is dealing with single adults who marry. Some have a hard-and-fast rule that the minute singles marry, they are not only not welcome to attend any meetings or functions of the single adult ministry, but they are actually forbidden to do so. This is not a wise position to take. Some single adults come to a church and join a single adult ministry when they are broken and barely alive emotionally and spiritually. With help, they put their lives back together again. In the process, they form friendships. Other members in the ministry become like family to them. To "excommunicate" them from the ministry just because they get married is unkind and unnecessary.

First, their reasons for wanting to attend are not so they can date someone else! They are in love with each other and just want to continue to be with their families and friends. Second, they will most likely phase themselves out of the single adult ministry on their own. It will be a natural process. They no longer need divorce or grief recovery, seminars on single living or single parenting, or socials. Their interests as a new family will grow and develop and include other married couples. The transition will occur; let it happen naturally.

EVALUATE YOUR MINISTRY

The secret of managing an effective ministry is to stay ahead of problems and take preventive rather than corrective action. At least every six months, evaluate each aspect of your single adult ministry.

- Use the questions provided at the end of each chapter in this book. These questions will help you evaluate your effectiveness in one specific area of ministry. Strong leaders will want to constantly evaluate their ministries.

- Develop a questionnaire and have your single adults provide you with feedback about each area of your ministry.

- Take your leaders away for a weekend or a Saturday and evaluate together through discussions and sharing of ideas. Consider revitalizing your ministry by taking a new approach, trying a new format, or starting a new program.

LOOK AHEAD

There are many challenges left for us to face in the field of single adult ministry. Dr. Bill Flanagan of St. Andrew's Presbyterian Church in Newport Beach, California, offers a list of the issues that are as yet unresolved in single adult ministry. You may be facing some of these right now, and your efforts will be a part of the eventual solutions.

Questions to consider:

1. How do we create a sense of genuine community in a basically mobile, transient group such as single adults?

2. How can leaders maintain their spiritual discipline over the long haul?

3. How do we teach absolute truths in a world where everything is treated as relative? (i.e., sexual ethics)

4. How do we determine the content and style of the teaching? (Do we teach topically, exegetically, expositorily, systematically? Do we teach only from the Bible, use curriculum, or study Christian books?)

5. How do we deal effectively with "problem people" or persons with ongoing special needs?

6. How do we discipline and restore leaders who have fallen?

7. How do we relate to insensitive colleagues who neither appreciate nor understand our visions for single adult ministry?

8. How do we broaden the perspectives of our single adults to include world missions?

9. How do we respond to single adults who are admittedly homosexual, with or without the commitment to not practice that lifestyle? How do we relate to individuals who occasionally (or frequently) break their commitment to celibacy?

10. How do we respond to single adults who are heterosexual and do not make a commitment to celibacy yet continue to attend our groups and seek positions that allow them to become actively involved?

11. How do we increase our ability to network with other leaders in single adult ministry, first in our cities, then in the United States, and finally internationally?

12. Which spin-off ministries are appropriate for inclusion in a single adult ministry or in the church as a whole? (Recovery, Remarrieds, Single Parenting, Outreach to Homosexual Christians, Victims of Abuse groups, Twelve Step programs, etc.)

13. How do we get more single adults on church boards, committees, search committees, and in positions of leadership such as deacons or trustees?

14. How do we get ministers with single adults to view this as a calling and not as a stepping stone to a "higher" position such as senior pastor, executive pastor, pastor of adult ministries, etc.?

15. How do we strengthen our premarital counseling and our family counseling to perhaps decrease the number of divorces?

16. How do we strengthen our ministry with single adults over 50, which are increasing in numbers?

17. How do we build single adult ministries that attract and meet the needs of single adults under 30 who are disillusioned with the realities of life today?

And these are only the beginning of the questions. There are more. As we resolve these, there will always be challenges just ahead of us. In order to keep ahead, we must continually address the issues of both the present and the future.

Appendix A

A BIBLICAL BASIS FOR MINISTRY WITH SINGLE ADULTS AND THEIR FAMILIES

When we look into the Scriptures, we find that God's design for the community of faith includes caring for one another, providing for one another, and reaching out to those for whom families are lacking.

HISTORICAL BACKGROUND

When God created Adam and said that it was not good for man to be alone (Gen. 2:18), He underscored the fact that people need other people. God then created Eve to be Adam's help meet and partner. God instituted the family as He instructed Adam and Eve to be fruitful and multiply and fill the earth. Families would include a husband, a wife, and children. Family members would take care of each other, provide for one another, and form strong bonds of emotional support and commitment with one another before God (Gen. 2:24).

God's ideal pattern for families was broken quickly. Adam and Eve disobeyed God, Cain killed his brother Abel, and the human race began a long history of not caring for one another in the way God had set up as the ideal. Marriages did not always last, and divorce became an early reality (Lev. 21:14). Still, the basic laws of God for a social order revolved around family relationships. It was through the family relationship that one inherited land or gained a portion of goods. Families took care of their members. Fathers provided for and protected their children and their wives.

But there were some people for whom the social order did not provide. God made special provisions to protect and provide for these five groups: strangers (foreigners who had embraced Judaism,[1]) the poor, the oppressed, widows, and orphans.[2] Throughout the Old Testament, combinations of these groups of people are singled out for God's unique intervention, protection, and provision. A sixth category of people, the Levites, were included in God's unique provision when it came to the distribution of the special tithe at the end of each third year (Deut. 14:28–29).

A SPECIAL SOCIAL ORDER

Because the ideal social structure, the family, excluded persons who did not have intact families (widows, the divorced, and orphans) and those who had no portion because they were resident foreigners (strangers), God established a different system to take care of them. Psalm 68:5–6 says that the Almighty becomes a father to the orphans, a protector of widows, and that He will place the solitary ones in families. The term "solitary" refers to those people who have no families or any other persons to help them.[3] This term includes single adults, both men and women.

The special social order or structure God set in place made sure the community of Israel reached out and cared for those who had no families. In addition, God would assume many of the missing family roles such as protector, reliever, deliverer, and provider.

Widows

The term *widow* as used in the Old Testament is broad, including not only the woman who had no husband because of death but also the woman who had been discarded, divorced, bereaved, and forsaken.[4] The Hebrew term *alamanah* refers to any woman, formerly married, who had no means of financial support or no male relative to take care of her. She was in need of special legal protection.[5]

In the Old Testament, there is sometimes a distinction made between widows who have other family members but not a husband and the more general term for a formerly married woman. In some verses, the divorced woman is listed separately from the woman who is widowed by the death of her husband, but it is clear that the term *widow* does not always refer just to the latter.

In 2 Samuel, we read that when King David regained his throne after the death of Absalom, he put away the 10 concubines whom he had left to keep the house when he fled from Jerusalem (2 Sam. 16:21–22).

David did not lie with them again because Absalom had had sexual relations with these women. David fed them and took care of them, but he kept them shut up until they died (2 Sam. 20:3). They lived the rest of their lives in "widowhood" (*alamanuwth*).[6]

Israel was called the wife of Jehovah from the time the nation was delivered from Egypt (Jer. 31:32), but it was labeled an adulterous wife because of the lack of faithfulness to Jehovah. Hosea wrote about how the adulterous "wife" was put away from Jehovah (Hos. 2:1–13). Isaiah prophesied about the subsequent restoration of the wife of Jehovah. He gave the promise from God that although Israel was a "woman forsaken," she would no longer remember the reproach of her "widowhood" (Is. 54:4–6).

In the New Testament, the term used for "widow" is *chera*, which means one lacking a husband, literally or figuratively a widow.[7] It is possible, therefore, that the term also refers to a formerly married woman who no longer has a husband whether or not her former husband is dead.

Orphans

The Old Testament term *fatherless* and the New Testament term *orphan* refers to those who do not have the protection of a father/parent, the lonely, and figuratively, for those bereft of a teacher, guide, or guardian.[8] These comprise another group with special needs that God has promised to meet.

The Hebrew people recognized the need to care for the true orphans (those whose parents had died or foundlings abandoned by their parents).[9] A child who had no father/parent to provide protection or to argue for his or her rights was to be given special consideration and treated gently. Such children were taken in and cared for, but they would not necessarily be given an inheritance. In the case of foundlings, there were specific rules about whom the orphan could marry because of doubt about the child's parentage. This was partly because of a fear of incest.

Strangers, the poor, and the oppressed (men and women)

Strangers (resident foreigners who had converted to Judaism) who had no inheritance, portion, or families came under the special social order. God made specific rules for dealing with these people to protect their legal rights and provide for their needs. These are explained in the section "Instructions for the Treatment of Widows and Others."

The poor, those who were unable to provide adequately for themselves, also came under God's special set of rules. How a person came to be poor—whether through misfortune such as pestilence or crop failure, mismanagement of resources, or the lack of an inheritance—was not the issue. The issue was that the poor needed to be protected and provided for.

The Levites

God provided for the Levites through a portion of the tithes each third year because they had no portion among the Israelites (Deut. 14:29).

GOD'S UNIQUE PATRONAGE

In several passages of Scripture, God states that there will be special relationships for the categories of people with special needs. God is: a helper to the orphans (Ps. 10:14); a righteous judge for the orphans and oppressed (Ps. 10:18); an executor of justice for orphans and widows (Deut. 10:18); a defender of the poor and orphans (Ps. 82:3); a reliever of the orphans, oppressed, and widows (Ps. 146:9; Is. 1:17); one who is ready to hear the cry of the orphans and widows (Ex. 22:22–24); a protector of the orphans and widows (Jer. 49:11); a giver of mercy to the orphans (Hos. 14:3); one who lifts up the poor and gives them an inheritance (1 Sam. 2:8); a giver and protector of the rights of the poor (Job 36:15); a refuge of the poor and oppressed (Ps. 9:9; 14:6); a provider of goodness for the poor (Ps. 68:10); one who loves the stranger (Deut. 10:18); one who promises that the poor will inherit the kingdom of God (Luke 6:20).

In other words, God uses divine omnipotence to be all-sufficient to orphans, widows, the poor, the oppressed, and strangers.[10] Also, as judge, God vindicates those widows who are distressed and in need of help.[11]

INSTRUCTIONS FOR THE TREATMENT OF WIDOWS AND OTHERS

God gave special instructions to His people for the treatment of widows and others. During harvest, they were to leave the dropped sheaves for widows, strangers, and orphans (Deut. 24:19). Late ripening olives were to be left on the branches for widows, strangers, and orphans (Deut. 24:20). Grapes left on the vines or on the ground after harvest were for widows, strangers, and orphans (Deut. 24:21). Widows, strangers, orphans, and Levites were to partake of the third-year tithes (Deut. 14:29; 26:12–13) and of the freewill contributions made during the Feast of Weeks (Deut. 16:10–11).[12] Strangers were to have the same protection under the law as the Israelites, and rights and rules were to be applied equally to both groups (Ex. 12:49; Lev. 19:34; Num. 15:16, 29). Strangers were to be loved as if they were Israelites (Lev. 19:34; Deut. 10:19). The rights of strangers were to be protected (Ex. 22:21). The fruits of the land during each seventh year were to be left for the strangers and the poor (Ex. 23:10–11; Lev. 25:6). During the year of Jubilee, the forfeited possessions of the poor were to be returned (Lev. 25:28). God's children were to be compassionate and give to the poor (Deut. 15:7–8). Often these instructions carried with them a promise that compliance would

both please and curry favor with God (Jer. 7:6–7).

In addition to the provisions God instituted for widows and others, there were also many prohibitions to be observed. They were not to keep the garment of a widow or the poor for a pledge (Deut. 24:12–13, 17). Widows, orphans, the poor, and strangers were not to be oppressed (Ex. 22:21; 23:9; Lev. 19:33; Deut. 24:14; Zech. 7:8–10). The fields of orphans were not to be entered forcibly (Prov. 23:10). Orphans were not to be robbed or taken advantage of (Deut. 24:17). Orphans and widows were not to be afflicted (Ex. 22:22–24).

Violations of these prohibitions carried promises of negative consequences. God's anger would wax hot (Ex 22:22–24). Those who didn't do right by the stranger, orphans, and widows would be cursed (Deut. 27:19). And Isaiah said "Woe to those who ... deprive the poor of their rights and withhold justice from the oppressed of my people, making widows their prey and robbing the fatherless" (Is. 10:1–2). Job said that there is no defense before God for those who have let the orphans go away hungry while eating their fill or causing harm to the widows (Job 31:16–17).

The Israelites were to take care not to hurt a widow because she had a broken spirit. Widows were to be spoken to gently, shown respect, spared bodily or mental grief, and their property was to be protected more carefully than one's own.[13]

In the days of the early church, the Hebrew Christians were criticized by the Greek Christians for not taking adequate care of their widows during the daily distributions of the alms and food (Acts 6:1).[14] It is evident from this passage that the expectation of caring for those who had special needs was still a part of the Jewish tradition. This practice, which was carried over and continued into the new Christian way of life, was regarded as more than a Jewish tradition but as God's revealed will for caring for those in need.

In Paul's first letter to Timothy (5:3–16), he gives several instructions that reinforce an attitude of caring response to widows. If a widow had a family who could care for her, she was to be taken care of by them, for this was pleasing to God. If anyone did not care for those family members who needed help, such as widows, that person would be worse than an infidel in God's sight. The failure to care for the widow would be seen as a denial of the faith. If a widow did not have any family to care for her, then the church was to take that responsibility and provide for her. Widows over the age of 60 could be taken into the church in a special way, to be of service to the church, as a kind of a female presbytery.[15]

James 1:27 states that pure religion is "to look after orphans and widows in their distress," which indicates there is a definite responsibility to reach out in a practical way to help these people.

God gave many instructions to His people about the treatment of all children (including orphans). Children were said by the psalmist to be a gift from God (Ps. 127:3). Children were to be well-trained and educated. Their early education was from their mothers (Prov. 31:1; 2 Tim. 1:5; 3:15), and fathers (or tutors) took over the education of the boys sometime after their fifth birthday (2 Kings 10:6). This education included not only basic reading and writing but also instruction in the Law of God and Hebrew practices (Ex. 12:26–27; 13:8, 14–15; Deut. 4:9; 6:6–7, 20–25; Prov. 6:20; 22:6).[16]

Jesus taught that children were to be treated gently and with love. When people brought little children to Him and were rebuked by the disciples, Jesus was displeased. He took the little children up in His arms and blessed them. Then He instructed the disciples not to forbid the children from coming to Him, for of such was the kingdom of God (Mark 10:13–16).

Paul, writing to the Ephesians, reminded fathers not to provoke children to anger but to bring them up in the nurture and admonition of the Lord (Eph. 6:4).

When speaking of the way strangers were to be treated, God expressed love for the stranger. He promised to provide food and clothing for those (men and women) who had no one to provide for them because they were not native, land-owning members of Israel (Deut. 10:18). When outlining the rights of the stranger, God's instructions were unparalleled in ancient legal systems because strangers were to be given legal protection just like the Israelites. God reminded the Israelites that they needed to remember that they were once strangers in Egypt. They should treat strangers among them as they would have wanted to be treated by the Egyptians (Lev. 19:33–37). Israelites were taught to be hospitable to strangers as a religious duty and to go to any lengths to protect their guests (Gen. 19:1–11; Judg. 19:16–30).[17]

It is evident that, both historically and scripturally, we are to reach out to men and women (widows, strangers, orphans, the poor, and the oppressed) with loving action, provide for them, and care for them.

It is also worthy of note that caring for people did not only mean providing for their physical needs. True, God made provision that they would be provided food and clothing. However, the full range of human need (as outlined by sociologist Abraham Maslow) was addressed.

Security needs were ensured as Jehovah made provisions that the legal rights would be zealously guarded for these people and as He instituted prohibitions such as not forcibly invading the fields of orphans. Social needs were considered, such as the need to belong, to be loved (Lev. 19:34), and to be included in the fellowship. These groups of people were specifically cited as being a part of the celebrations and gatherings of the community (Deut. 16:11; Deut. 31:12). Self-esteem needs of these groups were considered when God gave them the specific right to the harvest of the corners of the fields and the gleanings, the late-ripening olives, and the remaining grapes. This precluded them from merely receiving charitable gifts. This portion of the harvest was *theirs*, given to them by God through the community of Israel. Also, the dignity and self-esteem of the poor and widows was protected when God said that their clothing could not be kept as a pledge for a loan. Thus they could sleep in their own clothes/bedding (Deut. 24:12, 13, 17). The contribution (self-actualizing) needs were provided for as these groups of people became a part of the overall community of Israel even though they were not part of the normal family structure.

CURRENT APPLICATION

In biblical times God's people were to care for those who stood outside of the family unit (widows and orphans), for those who were strangers (the ones who did not belong), the poor, and the oppressed. The society/community in which these people lived was to take care of them under God's special patronage.

Who are those today who stand outside the family unit in our society and are in need of care? If we look closely, we will see that it is these same groups of people. However, the American culture/community is not responsive to taking care of these people for a variety of reasons, most of which include a lack of a national desire and willingness to be obedient to God's directives. Therefore, the church must step in to fill this need.

American culture is significantly different from God's created order. In biblical times, generations of extended families took care of one another, people lived most of their lives in one geographic location, and had long-term, close friends. Instead of living with their parents, being protected and cared for until marriage, young men and women today usually opt to—or are expected to—become self-supportive and move out of their parents' home after graduation from high school or college. Very few young people have positions waiting for them in a family business or inherit parcels of land that will support them when they are expected to be on their own. Many earn minimum wage and live at the poverty level. Add to their number the large percentage of unemployed and the economic realities of today, and one will find that there is a new generation of poor. Some are young people. Some are homeless single adults or families. Some are single parents with custody of young children. Some are formerly married men now trying to support themselves while paying child support and alimony to a former wife.

The search for jobs, or the jobs people do, may take individuals far away from their families and friends. We are a highly mobile society. We have become a nation of virtual strangers. Some of those who do not live close to biological families and long-term close friends are married and have begun their own families. They have some emotional and psychological support and, in the case of the two-income family, some financial support. But the single adult or single parent who is alone can be very much the lonely stranger.

Among us are many who are oppressed—their rights are being denied. Unborn children are aborted, and large groups of people are discriminated against because of their color, race, sex, or marital status—anything that deviates from "the norm." Regardless of the results of the national census and the predictions of sociologists, the American family norm is still two married parents living together with a couple of children. The father works outside the home, and the mother stays home to care for the house, the children, and the husband. If this norm ever was accurate, it is no longer accurate today. However, because the perception has not changed significantly, many single and single-again adults have told me that they are still seen as being outside "the norm." Never-married men (and sometimes women) over 30 are often suspected of being gay. Never-married women are considered "unclaimed blessings" and suspected, along with younger widows and divorced women, of being interested in any attractive married man. Singles, especially those who are divorced, are often prohibited from serving in leadership capacities within the church.

Widows in our society, those formerly married women (divorced or widowed), still need our ministry. In some cases, the needs are physical, just as it was in the days when God first gave the instructions on how widows ought to be treated. Physical needs include housing, food, clothing, transportation, assistance with difficult tasks, and money. Sometimes their needs involve the protection of rights and assistance with the legal system. However, the newly single-again adult has additional needs such as emotional support, recovery assistance, and regaining self-esteem. All single-again women have social needs for fellowship, spiritual needs for maturing in the faith, and achievement needs to be creatively involved in making a difference in the world. The church needs to be a catalyst for meeting some of these needs while still fulfilling its primary mission of evangelizing the lost.

However, if we reach out only to women who were formerly married, we will be ignoring or minimizing the men who were formerly married.

The emphasis on the special protection of widows in the Old and New Testaments reflects the cultural situation of that time. In the ancient world, the woman was referred to as either some man's daughter or another's wife. Women were subject to male authority.[18] Therefore, the special provisions God made for widows were to take care of those women who had no family, no male person to take care of, protect, or provide for them. Today, while there may be some needs unique to women who were formerly married, most of the basic needs of the formerly married are not gender specific. Men have these needs also.

Part of the reason for this is that men no longer can count on an inherited income-producing business or parcel of land that will ensure their economic survival. Today's men and women can be equally adrift once they must provide for themselves and are no longer living in the parental home. Some can find jobs that will support them. Others go for long periods of time unemployed, searching for a way to make financial ends meet. Therefore, our ministry with the formerly married has appropriately been expanded to include men as well as women.

Additionally, in modern society there is a large number of single adults who have never been married. They are no longer the responsibility of their parents, yet they have no families, no spouses. They experience some of the same needs as the formerly married in trying to live in a world primarily designed for couples and families. Some are single by choice and some because they've not found a mate they want who also wants them. Therefore, ministry with single adults must also include the "one-unit family."[19]

One of the functions of a successful ministry with single adults is working with the children of single adults. These children in many cases have been deprived of having two parents actively involved in their lives. They are "partial orphans." Even those who still have contact with both parents have difficult adjustments to make when moving from a two-parent family to a one-parent family (or sometimes *two* one-parent families). Because one or both of their parents usually will remarry, these children may face the challenging adjustment of living with or visiting a stepparent or stepsiblings. These changes in their lives often cause children great emotional distress. The church needs to consider these children and reach out in love to them.

If we are to take seriously God's instruction to reach out to others, particularly those who do not have families to care for them, the church must design effective ministries with single adults and their families. The church at large may reach out to some of these groups such as strangers (foreigners, "boat people," and non-English speaking groups within the community), the poor (needy or homeless families or the unemployed), and those whose rights are not being protected (unborn children, Third World populations, and those being discriminated against).

Ministries with single adults and their families focus in unique ways on widows, formerly married men and women, never-married adults, orphans (children who have lost one or both parents or whose parents no longer live together), strangers (men and women who have no families to care for them), the poor (single adults who are struggling to make ends meet, especially single parents with custody of minor children), and the oppressed (single adults who are not being accepted by the church at large because of their divorce or their illegitimate children).

Ministries with single adults and their

families is one way the church can carry out God's special patronage to those who might otherwise get lost, feel abandoned, or feel like strangers. When we minister with single adults and their families, the church becomes their new family, continuing the special social order God mandated for all of us.

APPENDIX A NOTES

1. George Foot Moore, *Judaism*, (Cambridge: Harvard University Press, 1944), 416.

2. Ibid., 164.

3. Robert Jamieson, A. R. Fausset, and David Brown, *A Commentary, Critical, Experimental, and Practical on the Old and New Testaments*, (Grand Rapids: William B. Eerdmans Publishing Company), 2-I:239.

4. James Strong, *The Exhaustive Concordance of the Bible, Dictionary of the Hebrew and Greek Words*, (Nashville: Abingdon Press), 13.

5. *Encyclopaedia Judaica*, (Jerusalem: Ketter Publishing House Jerusalem Ltd., n.d.), 487.

6. Matthew Henry, *Matthew Henry's Commentary on the Whole Bible*, (McLean: MacDonald Publishing Company, n.d.), 2:551.

7. Strong, 77.

8. Merrill F. Unger, *Unger's Bible Dictionary*, (Chicago: Moody Press, 1957), 814.

9. Meyer Berlin and Josef Zevin, eds., Harry Freedman, trans., *Encyclopedia Talmudica*, (Jerusalem: Talmudic Encyclopedia Institute, 1974), 297; and Francine Klagsburn, *Voices of Wisdom: Jewish Ideals and Ethics for Everyday Living*, (New York: Pantheon Books, 1980), 173–75.

10. Henry, 3:485; and James Orr, John L. Nuelsen, Edgar Y. Mullins, Morris O. Evans, and Melvin Grove Kyle, eds., *The International Standard Bible Encyclopedia*, (Grand Rapids: William B. Eerdmans Publishing Company, 1952), 5:3084.

11. Jamieson, Fausset, and Brown, 2-I:239.

12. *Encyclopaedia Judaica*, 487.

13. Berlin and Zevin, 427–431.

14. Jamieson, Fausset, and Brown, 3-II:32; and Unger, 1166.

15. Jamieson, Fausset, and Brown, 3-III:495.

16. Unger, 193.

17. Orr, Nuelsen, Mullins, Evans, and Kyle, 2865.

18. David Noel Freedman, Gary A. Herion, David F. Graf, John David Pleins, and Astrid B. Beck, eds., *The Anchor Bible Dictionary*, (New York: Doubleday, 1992), 948–956.

19. Ann Alexander Smith, *How to Start a Single Adult Ministry*, (Nashville: Sunday School Board of the Southern Baptist Convention, 1980), 7.

Appendix B

RESOURCES FOR SINGLE ADULT MINISTRY

The following is a list of available resources for ministry with single and single-again adults and children. Check your local bookstore for the latest offerings.

CHILDREN OF DIVORCED PARENTS

Dycus, Barbara. *God Can Heal My Owies.* 1199 Clay Avenue, Winter Park, FL 32789. Leader's guide for ages 2–6.

———. *God Can Heal My Hurts.* 1199 Clay Avenue, Winter Park, FL 32789. Leader's guide for ages 7–12.

Dycus, Jim, and Barbara Dycus. *Children of Divorce.* Elgin: David C. Cook, 1987.

DIVORCE RECOVERY

Peppler, Alice Stolper. *Divorced: Surviving the Pain.* St. Louis: Concordia, 1993.

Reed, Bobbie. *Life After Divorce.* St. Louis: Concordia, 1993. Book with leader's guide in back.

———. *Prescription for a Broken Heart.* San Diego: SAMA, 1982. (Not available in bookstores. Order from 7484 Carrie Ridge Way, San Diego, CA 92139, $5.)

Smith, Harold I. *I Wish Someone Understood My Divorce.* Minneapolis: Augsburg, 1986.

Smoke, Jim. *Growing Through Divorce.* Eugene: Harvest House, 1976. Book with leader's guide in back.

Splinter, John P. *The Complete Divorce Recovery Handbook.* Grand Rapids: Zondervan, 1992.

REMARRIAGE

Reed, Bobbie. *Merging Families.* St. Louis: Concordia, 1992.

SINGLE ADULT MINISTRY

Graver, Jane. *Single But Not Alone.* St. Louis: Concordia, 1983.

Hensley, J. Clark. *Coping with Being Single Again.* Nashville: Broadman, 1991.

Mitchell, Marcia. *Spiritually Single.* Minneapolis: Bethany House, 1983.

Petersen, Randy, and Anita Palmer. *When It Hurts to Be Single.* Elgin: David C. Cook, 1988.

Smith, Harold Ivan. *Positively Single.* Wheaton: Victor Books, 1986.

———. *Single and Feeling Good.* Nashville: Abingdon, 1987.

———. *Singles Ask.* Minneapolis: Augsburg, 1988.

Single Adult Ministries Journal. P. O. Box 62056, Colorado Springs, CO 80962-2056.

Single Adult Ministry Information (a newsletter). P.O. Box 11394, Kansas City, MO 64112.

SINGLE PARENTING

Brandt, Patricia, and Dave Jackson. *Just Me and the Kids,* Elgin: David C. Cook, 1985. Leader's guide.

Chisholm, Gloria. *Huddle Up.* Ada: Baker Books, 1991.

Gaulke, Earl H. *You Can Have a Family Where Everybody Wins.* St. Louis: Concordia, 1975. Christian companion book for Thomas Gordon's book, *Parent Effectiveness Training.*

Gordon, Thomas. *Parent Effectiveness Training.* New York: Wyden, 1970.

Hannah, Jane, and Dick Stafford. *Single Parenting with Dick and Jane.* Nashville: Broadman Press, 1993.

Reed, Bobbie. *Dear Lord, I Can't Do It All! Meditations for Single Mothers.* St. Louis: Concordia, 1993.

———. *I Didn't Plan to Be a Single Parent!*
St. Louis: Concordia, 1993.

———. *Single Mothers Raising Sons.* Nashville:
Thomas Nelson, 1988.

———. *The Single Parent Journey.* Anderson:
Warner Press, 1992.

Richmond, Gary. *Successful Single Parenting.*
Eugene: Harvest House, 1989.

Smith, Virginia W. *The Single Parent: Revised,
Updated & Expanded.* Old Tappan: Revell, 1983.

SINGLENESS

Dautenhahn-Richter, Elaine. *Single in Relationships.*
St. Louis: Concordia, 1983.

Foth, Gretchen. *Walking with Jesus.* St. Louis:
Concordia, 1986.

———. *How to Build and Nurture Christian
Friendships.* St. Louis: Concordia, 1986.

Reed, Bobbie. *The Single Adult Journey.* Anderson:
Warner Press, 1992.

Schroeder, Annette. *Single and Gifted.* St. Louis:
Concordia, 1986.

Weising, Edward F., and Gwen Weising. *Singleness:
An Opportunity for Growth and Fulfillment.*
Springfield: Gospel Publishing House, 1982.

White, William. *Single: Understanding and Accepting
the Reality of It All.* Anderson: Warner Press,
1990.

TWELVE STEP PROGRAMS

Knippel, Charles T. *The Twelve Steps.* St. Louis:
Concordia, 1994.

WIDOWHOOD

Branch, Roger G., and Larry A. Platt. *Resources for
Ministry in Death and Dying.* Nashville:
Broadman Press, 1988.

Kuenning, Delores. *Helping People Through Grief.*
Minneapolis: Bethany House, 1987.

Reed, Bobbie. *Prescription for a Broken Heart.* San
Diego: SAMA, 1982 (Not available in book-
stores. Order from 7484 Carrie Ridge Way, San
Diego, CA 92139, $5.00.)

Westberg, Granger E. *Good Grief.* Minneapolis:
Fortress, 1971.

NOTES

1. Russell Chandler, *Racing Toward 2001: The Forces
Shaping America's Religious Future*, (Grand
Rapids: Zondervan, 1992), 36.

2. Paul Petersen, "Let's Begin at Church," in *Single
Adult Ministry, The Next Step*, ed. Doug
Fagerstrom, (Wheaton: Victor Books, 1993),
90–92.